REGINALD POLE

By the same author

THE CONCERN FOR SOCIAL JUSTICE IN THE
PURITAN REVOLUTION

CARDINAL POLE

from a painting by a contemporary artist

REGINALD POLE

CARDINAL OF ENGLAND

by

W. SCHENK

LONGMANS, GREEN AND CO

LONDON ❖ NEW YORK ❖ TORONTO

LONGMANS, GREEN AND CO LTD
6 & 7 CLIFFORD STREET LONDON W I

ALSO AT MELBOURNE AND CAPE TOWN

LONGMANS, GREEN AND CO INC
55 FIFTH AVENUE NEW YORK 3

LONGMANS, GREEN AND CO
215 VICTORIA STREET TORONTO I

ORIENT LONGMANS LTD
BOMBAY CALCUTTA MADRAS

First published 1950

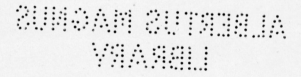
PRINTED IN GREAT BRITAIN
BY WESTERN PRINTING SERVICES LTD, BRISTOL

TO MY MOTHER

PUBLISHER'S NOTE

IT is with very deep regret that we record the death of Dr. Wilhelm Schenk on 18th June, 1949. *Reginald Pole* appears, therefore, without such final revisions as the author might have made in the page proofs, though we are sure, from our knowledge of the way in which Dr. Schenk worked, that, having corrected one set of proofs, he would be unlikely to make any but minor changes in the revised set. This book, then, is published in the form in which he left it, but unhappily it appears as the last of his works rather than as the second of a line of volumes of increasing breadth of subject and maturity of judgment.

PREFACE

CARDINAL POLE (1500–58) is little known in his native country. One of the reasons is obvious: Pole's chief intervention in English affairs—his attempt to restore Roman Catholicism under Queen Mary—was unsuccessful, and this failure was followed by the growth of the specific English horror of "Popery." Other reasons play their part too: Pole spent only eight years of his adult life in England but twenty-nine on the Continent, and his contribution to English history is therefore bound to be rather limited. For the Roman Church, however, his lifework has been of the greatest importance; he also has a place in the history of humanism. Seeing Pole properly means seeing him as a leading Catholic reformer and a European humanist.

Yet Reginald Pole was also a great Englishman of the sixteenth century, known abroad as the "Cardinal of England." He played his part in European life by carrying on a great English tradition—the tradition of Thomas More. Just as there was no conflict between More's English and European loyalties, until Henry VIII drove his cruel wedge between them, so it was Pole's chief aim to unite Europe and England in a renewed Christendom. But being nearly a generation younger than More, Pole was faced with a more difficult task.

The task itself was not clearly realized by Pole until More's martyrdom; he was among the first to whom More's death was a decisive, life-giving event. But in so far as this task involved public activities, he did not always shoulder it with the necessary determination. His nature drew him to the contemplative life, and the resulting conflict was one which he could never fully resolve. He was more successful in resolving the related conflict between humanism and Christianity. Here again he was greatly helped by More's example, and also by the vigorous Christian humanism prevailing among his best fellow-countrymen, as well as among the finest spirits of the Italian Renaissance.

Successively protégé and antagonist of his cousin Henry VIII, very nearly Pope, and at last Archbishop of Canterbury, Pole was in a unique position to *experience* the great issues of his time, and it so happens that he was a sensitive and honest man. Through a sympathetic consideration of his life we may be able to gain a closer insight into the tensions of the past; we may be able to re-live the fateful decisions of the sixteenth century by entering into a mind that was inescapably faced with them. Then it will appear of course that the tensions of the past are not really dead and gone but are still with us; "de nobis fabula narratur." The vitality of religion—the unity of Christendom—the relation between politics and religion—the problem of Christian humanism—the conflicting claims of action and contemplation: all these, to name only the dominant themes in Pole's life, are our concerns as much as Pole's. At this time of day a historical study may be excused for trying to establish this point. "Each epoch," we are told by Ranke, "stands in direct relation to God": and so it does, but to the same God.

I take this opportunity to acknowledge with gratitude the help I have received from many different quarters. Messrs. Longmans, with characteristic generosity, have enabled me to obtain valuable microfilms of the Pole MSS. preserved in the Vatican; in many other ways, too, they have spared no trouble to assist me and to ease my work. The Bodleian Library has contributed to the cost of these microfilms, in return for their being deposited in that library. The officials of the Biblioteca Apostolica Vaticana have done all they could to help me, and so have the particularly hard-pressed officials of the University Library at Göttingen. Like countless others, I have had the benefit of courteous and efficient assistance at the Public Record Office, the British Museum, and the London Library. In addition, I should like to thank the following librarians: the Rev. Dr. Jenkins and Dr. Irene Churchill, of the Lambeth Library; Mr. Hart, of the Inner Temple Library; Miss Crighton, of the Exeter Cathedral Library; and Messrs. Lloyd and Brockett, of the Roborough Library, Exeter. Mr. H. D. Wilson has helped me with the preparation of the MS. for the press. The University College of the South-West, Exeter, has covered some of my research expenses. The editors of *History* and the *Church Quarterly Review* have permitted me to use material published in those periodicals.

Of the more personal debts of gratitude I owe the greatest to Mgr. Dr. Hubert Jedin, of Rome. Mgr. Jedin has read the MS. and has given me invaluable advice on the problems of a period which he probably knows better than any other living historian. His friendly interest has been most encouraging. He has also put me in touch with two experts on the history of art—Dr. K. Rathe and Countess K. Lanckoronska—both of whom have most willingly helped me with the illustrations. My debt to Fr. Philip Hughes is hardly less great. He has read the MS. and has preserved me from many errors; his stimulating views have forced me to reconsider and improve substantial parts of the original text. Professor W. N. Medlicott has helped me more than he knows, by encouragement and consideration. Fr. Paul Brassell, S.J., has very kindly lent me his transcripts from the Vatican Archives. My friend Dr. Franz von Pollack-Parnau, of Vienna, has read the MS. and has put his astonishing knowledge of European history at my disposal. My brother's deep sympathy with the aims of all my work is a constant source of strength. My mother will know why this book is dedicated to her. Finally, I wish to thank my wife for her imperturbable criticisms, and even more for the prolonged hospitality she has extended to our common friend, the Cardinal.

W. S.

University College of the South-West,
  Exeter

October 1948

NOTES

ABBREVIATIONS:

Q. = *Epistolarum Reginaldi Poli S.R.E. Cardinalis et aliorum ad ipsum Collectio* (ed. Quirini, Brescia, 1744–1757, 5 vols.).

L. + *P.* = *Letters and Papers, Foreign and Domestic, of the Reign of Henry VIII* (ed. Brewer and Gairdner).

S.P. Ven. = *Calendar of State Papers, Venetian* (ed. R. Brown).

S.P. Span. = *Calendar of State Papers, Spanish* (ed. Bergenroth and others).

SPELLING AND PUNCTUATION of quotations in the text have usually been modernized.

CONTENTS

ILLUSTRATIONS

CHAPTER ONE

THE KING'S SCHOLAR
(1500–1527)

IT was the inescapable destiny of Reginald Pole to be either the friend or the foe of Henry VIII. He was doubly related to that King: his father, Sir Richard Pole, was a cousin of Henry VII, and his mother, Margaret Countess of Salisbury, was a Plantagenet.[1] Though their close relation to the Tudor monarchs was of great immediate value to the Poles, their connection with the ancient dynasty was of greater potential importance. A son of the Countess of Salisbury stood almost as near to the Crown of England as Henry VIII himself; at the time of the Tudors, whose claim to the throne was none too strong, a person of Pole's lineage would find it difficult to remain in the shelter of private obscurity. Yet, during the earlier part of Reginald's life (he was born in March 1500), his avoidance of public affairs seemed a real possibility, and one that he greatly cherished. He was not the eldest son of his parents; he was from the first destined for the Church; and he soon showed aptitude for such a career. His father died in 1505, when Reginald was only five years old, and at the age of seven the boy was sent to the grammar school of the Carthusians at Sheen near Richmond. We may assume that he was very happy there, as he retained a lasting affection for that place and that order. He may have seen something of the Court when it was at Richmond, his mother being a close friend of the Queen's, and his early impressions of Henry VIII, nine years his senior, must have been of the most pleasant kind. But such visits cannot have made up for the loss of the protecting warmth of family-life. After his time at the monastic boarding-

B

1

school he was sent to Oxford in 1512 or the year after, at the tender age of twelve or thirteen. There he was introduced, during a prolonged course of study, to some of the chief intellectual and spiritual tendencies of his age. The eight years he spent in Oxford were among the most formative of his life.

In the early years of the sixteenth century the University of Oxford began to respond more readily than before to the fertilizing influence of humanist ideas. Not that all dons were now becoming protagonists of the "New Learning"; there were plenty of dry-as-dusts, as there are in all universities, at all times. Nor should it be forgotten that much of the old-established curriculum continued to be taught and to be committed to memory, and that the traditional scholastic disputations continued to be staged, sometimes for several days on end. Nevertheless, in some circles at Oxford there was a fresh intellectual stirring, and when young Reginald Pole came up to Magdalen College it soon became clear that he would be connected with the new academic currents; of this, the names of his principal tutors, William Latimer and Thomas Linacre, were sufficient guarantee.

To the budding humanists of the day the study of Greek seemed of paramount importance. At first, this study could be successfully undertaken only in Italy where, in the second half of the fifteenth century, prominent Greek professors were teaching this language. In the late 1480's and early 1490's a small band of Oxford scholars spent some time in Italy learning Greek, and both Latimer and Linacre belonged to this group. Of Latimer we only know that he studied in Padua; Linacre, before taking his M.D. at Padua in 1496, made the acquaintance of Angelo Poliziano who introduced him to Lorenzo de'Medici. For a time Linacre even shared the teaching given to Lorenzo's sons by Poliziano and the celebrated Greek professor Demetrios Chalcocondylas. Both Linacre and Latimer seem to have returned from their travels as accomplished humanists. From now on they belonged to the five or six students of Greek in

2

England whose learning, according to Erasmus, surpassed even that of their Italian fellow-scholars.[2]

Reginald, the royal kinsman, was educated as the "King's scholar." The Pole family being then in great favour at Court, the King contributed to the educational expenses of the father-less boy. Henry paid him an exhibition of £12 in 1512 while Reginald was still at school, and in the following year Henry arranged for the prior of St. Frideswide in Oxford to pay a pension to "Reynold Pole, student in the University of Oxon-ford."[3] The gifted and well-educated young King was favour-ably inclined towards humanist studies and furthered the careers of humanist scholars by ecclesiastical preferment or various appointments at Court (Linacre, for example, became one of the King's physicians). When a wordy and violent conflict broke out in Oxford between "Grecians" and "Trojans" and one diehard savant denounced all supporters of Greek studies as heretics and devils, Henry, at the request of Thomas More, addressed a letter to the University in which he expressed the view that the students "would do well to devote themselves with energy and spirit to the study of Greek literature."[4] So it is not surprising that those prominent "Grecians," Latimer and Linacre, were destined to become the tutors of the "King's scholar" at Oxford.

As to the extent of Linacre's tutorship we may perhaps be a little sceptical, for Linacre was then living chiefly in London where he had an important medical practice and was busy preparing the foundation of the College of Physicians. But Latimer, who probably resided in Oxford at that time,[5] seems to have been Reginald's regular tutor, though the latter may also have had other tutors at Magdalen College where he had a separate apartment in the President's lodgings.[6] William Latimer has unfortunately left so little behind by which he can be judged that he must necessarily remain to us a rather shadowy figure. Perhaps the only feature of his character of which we can be reasonably certain is this very reticence based on what Erasmus wittily called "immodest modesty."[7]

Erasmus was quite right when he admonished him: "After the
funeral of the scholar, nothing comes to his heir, unless he has
committed his thoughts to Letters."[8] Latimer, whose scholarship was renowned in his lifetime all over learned Europe, can
therefore never be brought to life again.

For the same reason it is impossible to estimate Latimer's
influence on Reginald's growing mind. We may be certain
that Reginald received from him a thorough grounding in the
two classical languages, but for the wider influences we must
consider the general character of English humanism. What
was it that made these men turn to the study of Greek? The
answer, no doubt, would have varied a little in each case
(Linacre, for instance, used Greek chiefly for his medical
studies), but the main trend is unmistakable. It is the Erasmian
call "ad fontes": "Let him who desires to be instructed rather
in piety than in the art of disputation, first and above all apply
himself to the fountain-head—to those writings which flowed
immediately from the fountain-head,"[9] and after them, to the
Greek and Latin Fathers of the Church. To the English
humanists, the scholastic theology of their day appeared barren
and altogether devoid of truly religious significance. In addition
to this religious concern there was among them, to be sure, a
vigorous interest in "good letters," in style, and in civilized
living, but they did not consider this aspect to be of primary
importance (though, of course, important enough when the
silencing of obnoxious "Trojans" became necessary). John
Colet was indeed strongly opposed to the reading of all pagan
authors; "those books alone ought to be read," he taught,
"in which there is a salutary flavour of Christ."[10] This,
however, was an extremist opinion; a more representative
view is contained in Bishop Fox's Foundation Statutes for
Corpus Christi College, Oxford (1517), in which the Bishop
makes provision for the appointment of three public lecturers:
"One is to be the sower and planter of the Latin tongue," he
writes, "who is manfully to root out barbarity from our
garden." The second lecturer is to teach the Greek language,

for the sake of "good letters, and Christian literature especially." The syllabus of both these lecturers is to cover a wide range of classical authors, including Cicero, Virgil, Horace, Ovid, Homer, Sophocles, Aristotle, and "the Divine Plato." "Lastly," the Bishop concludes, "a third gardener, whom the other gardeners should obey, wait on, and serve, shall be the Reader in sacred Divinity, a study which we have always held to be of such importance as to have constructed this our garden for its sake, either wholly, or most chiefly."[11]

That this was not merely the pious wish of a learned bishop is borne out by the work of such men as John Colet and Thomas More. However different these two men may have been— Colet, solitary and stern, with Puritan leanings, "with no taste for poetry at all";[12] More, the centre of a large and loving family, fond of poetry, and always full of fun—there can be no doubt that both of them were religious figures of great significance, and that both of them intended their humanist interests to serve a primarily religious aim. As they were the two most famous English humanists of their time, young Reginald was bound to be influenced by their example. He himself said later that he and More had been on terms of familiarity and friendship.[13] We catch glimpses of him in two letters from More's correspondence dating from this period. From one of them, addressed to Oxford, it appears that Pole had asked his mother to make up a medicine for More who wrote to thank him for this kindness. In the other one More's daughter Margaret described Pole as "ut nobilissimus ita in omne literarum genere doctissimus, nec virtute minus quam eruditione conspicuus"—"as noble as he is learned in all branches of Letters, nor less conspicuous for his virtue than for his learning."[14] Such praise from More's favourite daughter must carry considerable weight. More himself must have felt that the young scholar would worthily carry on the tradition of Christian humanism.

The example of Colet may have reached Pole mainly through a fellow-scholar only five years his senior, Thomas Lupset,[15]

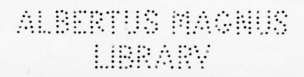

who as a boy had been educated in Colet's household and who, in 1519, became the second of Bishop Fox's classical lecturers at Corpus Christi. A few years earlier he had helped Erasmus in preparing the New Testament and the letters of St. Jerome. Though Lupset, as a lecturer in Greek and Latin, could hardly have been expected to share Colet's hostility to classical authors, he does seem to have preferred books on theology and philosophy to literary works.[16] In any case, the titles of his extant writings clearly indicate the real centre of his interests: "A Treatise of Charitie"; "An Exhortation to yonge men, perswadinge them to walke in the pathe way that leadeth to honeste and goodnes"; "A Compendious and a very Fruteful Treatyse, teachynge the waye of Dyenge well." Something of Colet's powerful moral teaching may well have been transmitted to Reginald by this earnest young man.

Another quality common to most of the prominent English humanists cannot have failed to imprint itself on Reginald's mind: their devout way of life. He may not have known the details of More's religious exercises,[17] but Colet's devotion was well known. And a further impressive example was even nearer at hand. That was the life of John Claymond, the President of Magdalen College during the earlier part of Pole's residence in Oxford, and from 1517 onwards the first President of the newly founded Corpus Christi College. Claymond was a distinguished humanist (though not, it seems, a Greek scholar), but first and foremost he was a priest. He used to sign himself "Eucharistiae Servus," because in the latter part of his life he received the Blessed Sacrament every day.[18] His contemporary biographer praises his temperance, his vigils, and his fasts. "During his frugal meals," we are told, "he was accustomed to read, pray, or attend to the various duties of his office." He liberally supported individual men of letters and several Oxford Colleges, and he was equally generous to the poor. "The poor friars of various orders, as well as the felons and debtors in Oxford gaol, were the constant recipients of his charity, no less than the needy inhabitants of Oxford and of the parishes in which he held livings."[19] This was the man in whose lodgings Reginald lived for several years.

Of Reginald's outward career at Oxford we know next to nothing. In June 1515 he took his B.A. Being then only fifteen years old, he can have mastered only the rudiments of learning, and there can be little doubt that he remained in Oxford until 1521, in which year he went to Italy. It seems, however, that he did not proceed to an M.A.; perhaps the prevailing dryness of the curriculum and his social position made him attach little importance to a degree. Thomas More's high praise suggests that Reginald was regarded by his elders as a most promising young scholar, and he showed by his subsequent career that these hopes were not ill-founded. Meanwhile Henry showered the usual ecclesiastical preferments on his gifted kinsman: in February 1518 he presented him to the collegiate church of Wimborne Minster, and a little later he conferred on him two prebends in Salisbury Cathedral. (Needless to add that Reginald was an absentee incumbent of all these benefices.) Finally, in February 1521, Henry sent him to Italy to continue his studies at the University of Padua, and gave him an allowance of £100 for the first year and probably a similar allowance annually.[20]

In going to Padua at this stage of his career Reginald followed the course taken by his teachers Linacre and Latimer and by many other English students before and after them. There had been English students of law and medicine in Padua at most times during the fifteenth century, and a little later such well-known men as Cuthbert Tunstall, Bishop successively of London and Durham, and Richard Pace, English ambassador to Venice, had finished their studies at that University. Reginald was now twenty-one. What precisely he had learnt in Oxford and what he was looking for in Padua, we do not know. But we may assume that he knew his Latin and Greek; that he had read fairly widely among the classical authors; that he shared the aversion of his fellow-humanists to the philosophy of the Schools; that the predominant ideals in his

7

mind had been, in one way or another, shaped by men like More, Colet, and Claymond; and that he hoped to test these ideals in the wider and richer world of Italian humanism.

Pole arrived in Padua in April 1521. He soon found out that as the kinsman of the King of England, who at that time was on very good terms with the Republic of Venice, he would not be allowed to lead the life of a private student. The Signory of Venice, to whom Reginald had been specially recommended by his royal cousin, and the magistrates of Padua treated him with the utmost respect, and he was generally sought after more than the other aristocratic students—"not on my own account," as he modestly adds himself, "but on account of the King who sent me."[21] It was his noble birth, too, that evidently facilitated his entering into correspondence with such humanists of world-wide fame as Pietro Bembo and Erasmus; both of these men were at pains to stress the excellence of Pole's ancestry in their first letter to him.[22] Pole was, in fact, obliged to live according to his station in life and, in a sense, to represent the King of England. He lived in a house that was large enough to shelter the English ambassador to Venice with all his retinue on his frequent visits to Padua, in addition to Pole's own "familia" of scholars and servants. All this was rather expensive, and Pole, in a letter to Henry soon after his arrival, expressed his anxiety lest the King should force him, for want of money, to abandon Padua for some obscure place in Italy.[23] It appears that, in spite of his income from his benefices and his allowance, Reginald found it difficult, as a friend put it, to maintain "the outward face of his reputation."[24]

The University of Padua, the heir to an ancient academic tradition and at that time virtually the State University of Venice, had been practically closed for eight years because of the Venetian wars (from 1509 to 1517), but soon afterwards it had recovered its former brilliance. It was mainly renowned, apart from its medical and legal schools, for the teaching of Greek and Latin eloquence and for the daring of some of its philosophers. The bold Pomponazzi had taught there until 1509—the philosopher who maintained, against Plato and against the Church, that the immortality of the soul could not be proved by reason. No such startling philosophical doctrines, however, seem to have been propounded in Reginald's time. Although we do not know, once again, what lectures he attended in Padua, we can form a fairly clear idea of his private tutor, Nicolo Leonico Tomeo.

Leonico, by now a man of sixty-five, had been Pomponazzi's colleague as Professor of Natural Philosophy and was a famous scholar, but, unlike Pomponazzi, he was not an original thinker. He has the distinction of having been the first Paduan professor to lecture on Aristotle and Plato from the Greek text, and it was as an interpreter of these two philosophers that he was best known. In addition to some commentaries on Aristotle, Leonico published a number of dialogues in the Platonic manner and partly on Platonic subjects.[25] From Leonico, we may be sure, Reginald could obtain an extensive and thorough knowledge of the two masters of Greek philosophy.

Reginald had brought with him an introduction to Leonico from his former tutor Latimer, who in his time had been Leonico's pupil himself. Leonico, in his first report to Latimer after little over a year, testified to Pole's immense zeal and great ability. "We have been able," he writes, "to get through some work. In the past sixteen months we have read together the eight books of Aristotle's Topicorum; four books De Caelo; and we have finished the first book De Generatione."[26] In 1523 Pole was joined by his friend Lupset who also became a pupil of Leonico, and in January 1524 Leonico was able to report: "Pole and Lupset are youths, me hercule! worthy of all praise. When they apply to the higher studies of letters, they make such progress that few are to be found their equal, and certainly none their superior."[27] In the same year Leonico dedicated his dialogues to Pole and mentioned in the dedication that Pole had read all works of Plato and Aristotle, as well as many commentaries on them. There can be no doubt that Pole made good use of his time in Padua.

So far we have watched Pole increasing his philosophical knowledge under the guidance of Leonico. But there were other matters, too, which claimed his attention. Soon after his arrival in Padua he made the acquaintance of the young French scholar Christophe de Longueil to whom he had an introduction from Thomas Linacre. Longueil, or Longolius, as he preferred to be called, took a liking to Pole and soon afterwards moved into his house; the friendship between the two young men (Longolius was only twelve years older than Pole) soon grew very strong. The personal history of Longolius is interesting both in itself and because it sheds light on some of the more questionable and even ludicrous aspects of Italian humanism.[28] Longolius, a native of Malines in the Netherlands, had studied in Paris and Poitiers and had become a French lawyer and a member of the Parlement of Paris. In 1517 he made the usual humanist pilgrimage to Italy and soon became associated with the humanist circles at the magnificent court of Pope Leo X, where the Papal secretary and poet Pietro Bembo reigned supreme in cultural matters. These men of refined taste regarded themselves as the heirs to ancient Rome: their master had replaced the Roman Emperor, they themselves were Roman senators, and the world was at their feet. Small wonder then that they felt entitled to confer on strangers, as of old, the citizenship of Rome. This was duly done in the case of Longolius, as a reward for a panegyric on the glory of Rome, past and present, and in 1519 Longolius became "civis Romanus." No sooner had this honour been conferred on the Gallic "barbarian" than another literary clique raised a violent protest. They discovered an earlier oration of Longolius, a panegyric on France, in which he had included some disparaging remarks about Rome. The next step was a charge of "lèse-majesté" and a pompous trial in front of the whole Papal Academy. It was probably mainly a mock-trial, a welcome entertainment for the Papal courtiers who, in spite or because of their sophistication, were often in danger of being bored, but Longolius took it seriously enough and left Rome for fear of assassination. The pageant, however, ended with the full rehabilitation of Longolius who returned to Italy and followed Bembo, on the latter's retirement from the Curia, to Padua where Pole met him in 1521. It was in Pole's house that Longolius, after a short illness, died only one year later, leaving his library to Pole, who wrote a short biography of his friend and published it together with Longolius' collected writings and letters.

Longolius, as was to be expected, had completely fallen for Bembo's extravagant imitation of ancient Rome. The literary expression of this pose was the dogma that the only Latin worth writing and reading was that of Cicero. On Bembo's instigation, Longolius took a solemn vow not to read any books for five years except Cicero's and never to use any words which could not be found in Cicero's writings.[29] This Ciceronianism gave rise to a protracted quarrel among humanists, but it was, in fact, decisively exploded in the very beginning by the level-headed and shrewd Erasmus who wrote in his sarcastic dialogue *Ciceronianus* (1528): "Cicero, the senator and proconsul, writes to men of his own rank about the efforts of the provincial commanders, about the battle-order of the legions; he points out the dangers, and predicts the outcome of events. When Longolius, imitating Cicero, writes similar things to his learned friends living in leisure, as if he were concerned about the highest matters, must not the affectation of it have a chilling effect [nonne friget affectatio]?"[30] Such common sense, however, was abhorred in the Ciceronian circles. For our purpose it is worth noting that Pole, in his biography of Longolius, does not sound the slightest critical note about his friend's doctrines and antics, duly recorded there; the biography itself is, indeed, written in faultless Ciceronian Latin.

Another remark of Erasmus' about the Ciceronians is very illuminating. "There is now in Rome," he says, "a certain fellowship of people who care more for literature than for piety."[31] There can be no doubt that this criticism of Medicean Rome and its Epicurean humanists was fully justified, in spite of the outward respect paid to the established religion. Though it is not necessary to believe that all members of the Papal Court lived grossly immoral lives, a charge of religious laxity and indifference cannot be rejected. Longolius, for instance, was not a libertine, but his life, according to his own description, was a round of refined sensuous pleasures and completely devoid of any religious exercise or meditation.[32] This atmosphere is admirably caught in a poem addressed to Longolius by his young and gifted friend Marc-Antonio Flaminio:

> But when the insect hum is still,
> And sunbeams rest on height and hill,
> We saunter forth, and climb the steep
> That beetles o'er the purple deep:
> And thence we drop the painted float,
> Or idly watch each little boat,
> That steals upon the tranquil bay
> With snow-white sail and pennon gay,
> And vainly wish our life may be
> As peaceful as yon blessed sea.[33]

This way of life, so tempting to the bright young men of the day and to their elders as well, was most influentially represented by the former leader of the humanist coterie at Rome, Pietro Bembo, who had now retired to his country house near Padua. There he continued to be the centre of an admiring group of disciples and friends, to which Reginald was admitted soon after his arrival in Italy.

Bembo belonged to a Patrician family of Venice. In his youth he travelled with his father, who was in the Venetian diplomatic service, and spent some time at the Medicean Court in Florence. Later, he lived for several years at the smaller but equally cultivated Courts of Ferrara and Urbino: in Ferrara he fell ardently in love with Lucrezia Borgia, while the ladies of Urbino received from him the polished, though somewhat high-flown, sermons on Platonic love immortalized

in Castiglione's *Cortegiano*.[34] We have already met him at the
next stage of his life—as the secretary of Leo X and "arbiter
litterarum" at the Papal Court. In Rome he began to live
with a beautiful girl called Morosina who bore him three
children and remained with him until her death. He wrote and
published a good deal of Italian prose and poetry. Most of it is
purely imitative, stilted, and rather dull; only occasionally a
more personal tone is audible, particularly when he gives
expression to his love for the country, as for instance in this
exhortation to Ercole Gonzaga, Duke of Ferrara:[35]

> *O Ercole, che travagliando vai*
> *Per lo nostro riposo, e'n terra fama*
> *E'n ciel fra gli altri Dei t'acquisti loco;*
> *Sgombra da te le gravi cure omai*
> *E qui ne ven, ove a diletto e gioco*
> *L'erba, il fiume, gli augei, l'aura ti chiama.*

> Oh Ercole who for our quiet's sake
> Workest laboriously, thou hast acquired
> Glory on earth, among the Gods a place;
> Now it is time to shed all grievous care:
> Come hither now, where to delight and play
> Are calling grass, brook, birds, the very air.

After his retirement from Rome, Bembo was in a position
to realize his dream of a life "procul negotiis," devoted to study
and enjoyment. Here is his own description of his life in his
Paduan villa: "I read and write as much as I like; I ride, I
walk, I often stroll in a spinney at the bottom of my garden.
From this pleasant and beautiful garden I sometimes gather
with my own hands the first-fruits for my supper, and some
mornings I collect a basketful of strawberries, which spread
their fragrance in my mouth and all over my table. I need not
mention that my house is full of roses all day long. I also
have the opportunity of using a boat on a graceful little stream
which passes my house and after a very short time flows into
the Brenta, a fine and serene river. The same river washes

my fields from another side, and so, going for a good walk of an evening, it is always water, rather than land, that delights me."[36] The villa itself resembled a museum. There were portraits of Dante, Petrarca, and Boccaccio, and a supposed likeness of Petrarca's Laura; a portrait of Bembo himself, by Raphael, and a picture by Mantegna; a number of female nudes; classical statues of marble and bronze, mostly representing mythological figures; ancient vases, medals of all sorts, richly mounted gems, numerous coins, and old inscriptions.[37] Bembo was also a collector of Greek, Latin, and Provençal manuscripts and possessed an extensive library. It was in this setting that Bembo received his friends and discussed with them the matters nearest to his heart: the excellence of Ciceronian Latin and the legitimate use of the vernacular in poetry. From this quasi-retreat he also conducted a vast correspondence, and he never allowed himself to lose sight of the political world that for him and his friends centred in Rome.[38]

This many-sidedness, it need hardly be stressed, has nothing in common with the efforts of the great "uomini universali" of the Italian Renaissance; Bembo was far too weak to attempt a genuine synthesis of the various spheres of experience. In town or country, at Court or in his villa, life was calling him merely "to delight and play," not to serious exertion or ascetic renunciation; asceticism of any kind is, indeed, the direct opposite to his way of life. Even in his philosophy, that elegant Platonism so elegantly propounded by him, this note of ultimate irresponsibility is unmistakable: philosophy is an additional adornment of life, not its centre and guide. It is for these reasons that both as a poet and a thinker Bembo is now dead. He is the true precursor of a cultural type well known among the educated classes of our own day: the sophisticated dilettante constantly searching for amusement, as if to conceal from himself and the world his inner emptiness.

Let it be repeated: Bembo was not a conspicuously immoral man (even his concubinage could be, and was, excused on the grounds that he had taken only minor orders), nor was his religious orthodoxy ever in doubt. Had it been otherwise, his influence on his respectable contemporaries could hardly have been so powerful. We do not know whether Pole's outward habits of life were influenced by his Epicurean friend; Lupset, at any rate, in a letter to Erasmus written from Padua, speaks of him in terms similar to those used by More, praising particularly his stability of mind and his moral probity.[39] But the atmosphere of the place could not have altogether passed him over, and it is significant that the only plan for original academic work that he seems to have conceived in Italy did not amount to more than a critical edition of Bembo's and Longolius' idol, Cicero.[40] And we can go further than that. The character of a young humanist was bound to be affected by the moral example of the famous men in his circle, in Italy as well as in England. The outstanding personality in Pole's Paduan circle was Bembo's, and in the absence of any criticism on Pole's part we must assume that, for a time at least, he shared the high esteem in which Bembo was held by his disciples. At this stage of Pole's life the example of Bembo must have been a temptation, all the more alluring for its seeming harmlessness.

It must not be assumed that Reginald spent all his time in Padua. Padua is not far from Venice, and Venice in the sixteenth century combined all the charm it still possesses with the attractions of a busy and wealthy capital. In view of his exalted rank Reginald could hardly avoid going to Venice on certain state occasions. On Corpus Christi Day, for example, when the Doge, "clad in cloth of gold with a crimson satin mantle and crimson ducal cap," heard Mass in St. Mark's Church, or on Ascension Day, when the Doge performed the ancient ceremony of "espousing the everlasting Sea," the young kinsman of the English king could not fail to be present. On Corpus Christi Day 1525 Reginald took part in the splendid procession (we know what it must have looked like from Bellini's picture), walking behind the ambassadors from the Pope, England, Austria, Milan, Ferrara, and Mantua, and together with the Venetian councillors and the Bishop of Paphos.[41]

The English ambassador, walking just in front of him, was among his close personal friends: it was Richard Pace, the humanist, friend of Erasmus, and secretary of Henry VIII. Pace had, in his day, studied in Padua, and during his term as ambassador in Venice he was naturally attracted to the Venetian university town where he often stayed as Pole's guest. Pace in his turn drew Pole and Lupset into the life of the colourful metropolis; it seems, in fact, that after 1523 Pole and Lupset spent more time in Venice than in Padua.[42] Pace introduced his young friends to the immensely complicated diplomatic affairs of the time, and in this way Pole became an eye-witness of some of the events preceding the fateful battle of Pavia (1525) between the two young monarchs Francis I, King of France, and the Emperor Charles V. It may well be that his insight into political matters, shown a few years later, dates from this period of his life.

In view of the cordial relations prevailing at that time between Henry VIII and the Papacy, it is remarkable that Pole did not go to Rome until 1525, and then only for a flying visit during the Jubilee festivities of that year and without asking for an audience with the Pope. This haste is rather suggestive. We might have expected the friend of the "Roman citizen" Longolius and the admirer of Bembo to have been duly impressed by the splendours of Medicean Rome. That this was not so is confirmed by Richard Morison, the English diplomat and publicist, whose word on this matter, despite his partisanship for Henry, need not be doubted. Morison, who was a member of Pole's household in 1535,[43] reports him as saying that when he had been in Rome "three or four days, and seen the abomination of the cardinals, bishops, and other their officers, with the detestable vices of that city, he could in no wise tarry there any longer."[44] There is nothing improbable in this reaction of a young man who, only twelve years later, was to take part in the drawing up of a famous proposal for

CHRISTOPHER LONGOLIUS

from an engraving by N. Larmessin

CORPUS CHRISTI PROCESSION IN THE PIAZZA OF ST. MARK, VENICE

from a painting by Gentile Bellini

radical Church reform, the "Consilium de Emendanda Ecclesia." Pace had expressed similar feelings in 1517 and may indeed have influenced Pole in this respect; he had strongly condemned the Rome of Leo X as "plainly monstrous, full of all shameful vice, devoid of all faith, honesty, and religion."[45] If Morison's evidence can be accepted we have in it an indication that the example of Pole's Italian teachers and friends would not make him forget the firm teaching of the great English humanists; that Longolius and Bembo were not to supplant Colet and More. Meanwhile, however, Pole had to return to his native country, and there he was to undergo a severe test of character, for which his education had not sufficiently prepared him.

NOTES TO CHAPTER ONE

[1] See Genealogical Tables, p. 174.

[2] *Opus Epistolarum Des. Erasmi Roterodami*, ed. P. S. Allen, vol. 1, p. 415.

[3] *L. + P.*, vol. ii, part 2, p. 1455; *L. + P.*, vol. i, part 2, p. 932.

[4] Erasmus in 1519: Allen, op. cit., vol. iii, p. 547. The translation and some details are taken from F. Seebohm, *The Oxford Reformers*, Everyman's Library, p. 287.

[5] He was incorporated M.A. in 1513: Wood, *Fasti Oxonienses* (1815), vol. i, p. 39.

[6] Wood, *Athenae Oxonienses* (1813), vol. i, p. 279.

[7] F. M. Nichols, *Epistles of Erasmus* (1904), part iii, p. 253.

[8] Nichols, op. cit., part iii, p. 257.

[9] Seebohm, op. cit., pp. 205–6.

[10] J. H. Lupton, *A Life of John Colet* (1887), p. 76.

[11] Statutes for Corpus Christi College, transl. by G. R. Ward (1843); translation slightly altered.

[12] Erasmus on Colet (J. H. Lupton, *Lives of Vitrier and Colet*, (1883), p. 42).

[13] Pole, *Pro Unitatis Ecclesiasticae Defensione* (1555), f. 21b. This book was written in 1535–6: cf. Chapter 4 of this study.

[14] T. Stapleton, *Tres Thomae* (1612), pp. 198–9. The actual wording is More's; and this was the impression made upon him by his daughter's letter to which he, in his turn, replied: "Explicare calamo non possum, vix etiam cogitatione complecti, quanta me voluptate perfuderunt elegantissimae literae tuae Margareta charissima. Aderat legenti iuvenis ut nobilissimus, etc."—"I cannot explain with the pen alone, and can scarcely comprehend in thought, how great a pleasure your elegant letter afforded me, dearest Margaret. As I read, the young man stood before me as noble, etc."

[15] Cf. J. A. Gee, *Life and Works of Thomas Lupset* (1928).

[16] Cf. the books he recommends to one of his students: Gee, op. cit., p. 13.

[17] For these, cf. R. W. Chambers, *Thomas More* (1935).

[18] Wood, *Athenae* (1813), vol. i, p. 104. An example of such a signature survives: *Oxf. Hist. Soc. Collectanea II* (1890), p. 60.

[19] T. Fowler, *History of Corpus Christi College* (1893), pp. 81–2.

[20] *Dictionary of National Biography*; *Q.*, vol. i, p. 5. Pole was probably no longer a layman: cf. below, Chapter 5, note 15.

[21] *L.* + *P.*, vol. iii, No. 198; vol. iv, No. 1529; *S.P. Ven.*, vol. iii. No. 184.

[22] *Q.*, vol. i, pp. 383, 394.

[23] *L.* + *P.*, vol. iii, No. 198.

[24] Lupset in 1529–30: Gee, op. cit., p. 288.

[25] *Nicolai Leonici Thomaei Opuscula* (1524); *Dialogi* (1524).

[26] F. A. Gasquet, *Cardinal Pole and his Early Friends* (1927), p. 34.

[27] Gasquet, op. cit., p. 53.

[28] Cf. Th. Simar, *Christophe de Longueil, humaniste* (1911). Twenty-five books which used to belong to Longolius are now in New College Library, Oxford: Allen, op. cit., vol. xi, pp. 379–83.

[29] *C. Longolii Orationes duae pro defensione sua*, etc. (1533), f. 9 b.

[30] Erasmus, *Opera* (Basel, 1540), vol. i, p. 854.

[31] Erasmus, loc. cit.

[32] Cf. e.g., a letter to Bembo, July 1520: *C. Longolii Orationes duae*, etc. (1533) f. 134 a.

[33] The translation from the Latin is contained in *Fifty Select Poems of M. A. Flaminio*, transl. by E. W. Barnard (1829), pp. 27–8.

[34] Book IV, chapters 51, 52, 57, 57, 68–70. Bembo's own dialogues *Gli Asolani* contain the same ideas in a similar form.

[35] Bembo, *Rime*, Sonetto XVII.

[36] Letter in 1525, quoted in V. Cian, *Un decennio della vita di M. Pietro Bembo* (1885), pp. 35–6.

[37] Cian, op. cit., p. 106.

[38] Cf. Cian, op. cit., p. 130.

[39] Allen, op cit., vol. vi, pp. 144–5.

[40] T. Phillips, *Life of Reginald Pole* (2nd ed. 1767), vol. i, p. 24.

[41] Sanuto's Diaries (February 25th, 1525), *S.P. Ven.*, vol. iii, No. 1042.

[42] Gasquet, op. cit., pp. 54, 65, 76, 87.

[43] *L.* + *P.*, vol. ix, No. 102.

[44] Richard Morison, *Exhortation to styrre all Englyshe men to the defence of theyr countrye* (London, 1539), fol. D.

[45] Quoted in A. F. Pollard, *Henry VIII* (1902), p. 162.

CHAPTER TWO

TEMPTATIONS
(1527–1532)

WHEN the King's Scholar, after an absence of six years, returned to England early in 1527, he might have been expected to take some part in public life, possibly at the royal court. But this, evidently, was not what Reginald intended to do. Instead, he withdrew to the Carthusian monastery at Sheen, where he had been educated as a boy, occupying the house which John Colet had built for himself within the precincts of that religious foundation. Colet had lived in it only a short time at the very end of his life; he had not been spared to enjoy a quiet evening after a busy public career. What part, if any, Colet and Pole were taking in the monastic routine is unknown. It must not be assumed that either of them wanted to become a monk. They probably attended some of the services and shared some of the meditative exercises, without being compelled to do so at all times. It has been pointed out that in this period of decline many monasteries fulfilled the functions of modern hotels and boarding-houses, and it was this kind of boarding-house that Pole rightly regarded as suitable for the continuation of his studies. But he was soon to learn that he would not be allowed to retire from the world in this comfortable way at the ripe age of twenty-seven; the King was in fact determined to draw him into the royal service.

The later outrages of Henry VIII should not be allowed to obscure his early promise. It is, fortunately, not our task to explain the decline, so impressively described by A. F. Pollard,[1] in Henry's moral and spiritual capacities. Here it must suffice

19

to remind ourselves that Castiglione had written of young Henry: "It seems that nature was willing in this prince to show her cunning, to combine in one body alone so many excellent virtues as are sufficient to deck out an infinite number."[2] Henry was bound to appear in this light to the author of the *Cortegiano*, for he was an accomplished wrestler, jouster, tennis-player, besides being a good linguist, an outstanding musician, and no mean theologian. He was interested in humanist scholarship and promised to encourage it; without learned men, he was reported to have said, "life would hardly be life."[3] No wonder, then, that the humanists' hopes were running high at Henry's accession. Erasmus, whom the King personally invited to England, was told by his friends that a Golden Age of scholarship was about to begin.

All this had happened quite a long time ago. Since then many of the earlier hopes had been disappointed. Henry's interest in the finer arts of life had turned out to be rather superficial; he had mainly indulged in an endless round of costly court festivities. The chronicle of his faithful adherent Edward Hall abounds in colourful descriptions of what must have been very colourful affairs—banquets, tourneys, and pageants of all kinds. "Against the day of the Epiphany at night," runs one of these reports, "before the banquet in the hall at Richmond, was a pageant devised like a mountain, glistening by night, as though it had been all of gold and set with stones, on the top of the which mountain was a tree of gold, the branches and boughs friezed with gold, spreading on every side over the mountain, with roses and pomegranates, the which mountain was with vices brought up towards the King, and out of the same came a lady, apparelled in cloth of gold, and the children of honour called the Henchmen, which were freshly disguised and danced a Morris before the King."[4] And so, in this somewhat garish manner, it went on year in year out, the King in the midst of it all, dancing, jousting, masquerading, making love, and eating and drinking hard (and therefore getting very fat). As the years went by he developed a taste for matters of state, but until 1529 their control remained chiefly in the hands of his all-powerful minister Thomas Wolsey, Cardinal and Archbishop of York.

Pole was not cut out for a "cortegiano," and Henry may not, indeed, have put any pressure on him to share this kind of court life. The King's main desire was probably to use his kinsman's gifts in the service of the state, or the church, or both. There were plenty of precedents for this in the careers of other English humanists. The King expected, not altogether unreasonably, that men of outstanding abilities, who had enjoyed the best education of their age, should eventually render some practical service to their country. Linacre, for example, became one of the King's physicians. Pace was an active diplomat, and afterwards Colet's successor as Dean of St. Paul's. Lupset, too, although he was at one time a University lecturer, was occasionally used by Henry in a quasi-diplomatic capacity.[5] Thomas More's public career is another case in point: the career of the humanist lawyer who was dragged to Court and into the various distinguished offices he held in the course of his life. And then there was the learned Bishop of London, Cuthbert Tunstall, a former student of Padua University and, according to Erasmus, one of the lights of English scholarship. Tunstall had accompanied More on an important embassy to the Netherlands; in the 1520's he had been sent to the Continent on several diplomatic missions; and in 1530 he was to be translated to the see of Durham, which, more than any other English see, involved the incumbent in duties resembling those of a viceroy.

All these men were well known to Pole; he must have realized that he was expected to follow the example of his fellow-humanists. We do not know Henry's precise intention, but there is an indication of it in the ecclesiastical preferment he selected for Pole in 1527: in that year Pole was made Dean of Exeter. Perhaps Henry intended to use him also for occasional diplomatic tasks, for which Pole's knowledge of foreign countries and international contacts would have been invaluable.

Pole, however, did not show any inclination to go to Exeter and to take up his benefice; like Bembo and so many other contemporaries, he was content to draw his revenue as an absentee incumbent, appointing a deputy to carry out his official functions. Nor—and this is perhaps even more surprising—did he avail himself of an opportunity to return to Oxford, afforded to him by his election, in 1524, as a Fellow of Corpus Christi College. It almost looks as if Reginald had tried to play truant during those years. But this was not to last very long; soon his mind began to be occupied with a conflict which was to burden him with irrevocable responsibilities and ultimately give a new direction to his life.

This was the time when "the King's great matter," as it was often referred to then, or the King's divorce, as we are used to calling it now, began to be the centre of English affairs. The immensely complicated facts of that *cause célèbre* are now well known and here they cannot be discussed at length, but some of them must be briefly recalled to see how the case was likely to affect a contemporary of Pole's standing. Strictly speaking, there was no divorce at all: the King maintained that his marriage with Katharine of Aragon had been invalid from the first because of Katharine's previous marriage to Henry's brother Arthur, who had died a few months after the wedding, at the age of fifteen. True, Pope Julius II had issued a special dispensation enabling Henry to marry his deceased brother's wife, but Henry eventually claimed that such a dispensation, being contrary to divine law, could not properly be given. In this connection it was relevant to know whether the earlier marriage of Katharine with the young and ailing Prince Arthur had been consummated, for only in that case could it be held to constitute an impediment for Henry's marriage. Katharine solemnly declared that her first marriage had not been consummated; to her friends and followers this was sufficient proof. Disregarding this, the King asked Pope Clement VII to annul his marriage with Katharine, in order to marry Anne Boleyn. It seems that Anne, unlike her sister Mary, refused to become

Henry's mistress and insisted on marriage, but in fairness to Henry it should be stated that his desire to have a legitimate male heir (he already had an illegitimate son) must have played an important part in this matter. Nor is it at all certain that he did not sincerely believe in the invalidity of his marriage with Katharine; he was superstitious, and the early deaths of all male children born to the Queen may have seemed to him a sign of divine wrath. It is all the more remarkable therefore that he was about to marry a woman who, on account of his illicit relations with her sister, stood in the same degree of affinity to him as Katharine. But then, people are not usually given to perfectly logical reasoning on such matters; for the most part they are quite ready to believe unflinchingly in the righteousness of their cause.

Pole could not have been expected to approve of the divorce project, as his mother was an intimate friend of Queen Katharine's and by now the trusted and beloved governess of Katharine's daughter Mary, the future Queen. It seems, however, that Pole took no part in the divorce proceedings on either side between 1527 and 1529. In the latter year, probably in order to be further away from the political scene, he applied to the King for permission to continue his studies abroad, this time at the University of Paris. This permission was granted, together with a payment of £100 "for one year's exhibition beforehand," and so we find Reginald travelling to Paris, accompanied by Lupset and other friends, complete with fustian mattresses, two hogsheads full of books, and virginals.[6] But soon after Pole's departure the King adopted a suggestion made by Thomas Cranmer (then an unknown Cambridge don, soon to become a protagonist in this drama) to consult the universities of Europe on the validity of his marriage. He made elaborate preparations to secure a favourable verdict from the members of the learned world, and he decided to test his kinsman's loyalty by asking him to act as the royal emissary to the theological faculty of the University of Paris.

We may well believe Pole's statement, made some years

later, that this royal order came as a great shock to him. He tried to excuse himself on the grounds of inexperience, and Henry therefore sent him an assistant (Edward Foxe, the future Bishop of Hereford) who conducted the necessary negotiations.[7] But it cannot be denied, and should not be concealed, that Pole, too, took some part in this business, however odious it may have seemed to him. Henry himself wrote to Pole on 18 June 1530: "To your dexterity and faithfulness we ascribe the furtherance of our cause," and an anonymous correspondent wrote to Pole in the same year: "Being at court, I was desired by the Duke of Norfolk to write to you how greatly he congratulated both himself and you that you acted so stoutly on the King's behalf."[8] We also have a letter of Pole's to Henry, of May 13th, in which he reports progress in the King's matter.[9] And during the proceedings on April 29th, the King paid Pole an additional sum of £70[10]—a payment which would be unintelligible without some action of Pole's on behalf of the King. Such action, whatever its precise nature, came perilously near to approval of the divorce, and it is quite understandable that the King continued to have hopes of persuading his kinsman to enter his service. We need not, of course, go so far as to assume that Pole took an active share in the bribery involved in this particular task; he probably left that to the more experienced Foxe.

It should be pointed out in passing that these proceedings shed a somewhat lurid light on the moral state of the European universities at that particular time. This is an aspect of academic history not usually dealt with by the historians of these ancient seats of learning. Not only the monasteries, it is obvious, were in dire need of reform. Then, as so often, professors were untrue to the deeper meaning that can be associated with their title. This is not to suggest that all those who declared in Henry's favour were bribed; Henry's case was not at all bad from a strictly legal point of view. But that there was a good deal of bribery is beyond doubt, and in the case of the French scholars the temporary friendship between their King and Henry probably counted for much. Pole may be excused for not attaching undue weight to the verdict of the universities; they are, he said politely understating the case, "often led by affections."[11] On this occasion, at any rate, the "res publica litterarum" did not show any marked sense of independence.

On 2 July 1530 this unsavoury business came to an end as far as Pole was concerned. On that day the long-awaited decree by the theologians of Paris was published, definitely stating that the Pope had no power to grant a dispensation for the marriage of a widow with her deceased husband's brother. Having achieved this, Pole was now recalled to England and arrived there in the course of July. Once again he tried to retire to the Charterhouse at Sheen, and once again the King tried to draw him into public life. This time, however, the King made more definite and more determined efforts.

A few days after Cardinal Wolsey's death (29 November 1530) the Duke of Norfolk, acting on behalf of the King, approached Pole with the offer of the now vacant Archbishopric of York. This was a signal distinction for a man of barely thirty and a sign of Henry's high esteem for his learned cousin. Only one condition was attached to this offer: Reginald had to declare his opinion on the divorce, for the King, as Norfolk put it, "did not wish to confer such a high honour on an adversary."[12] Now we shall see in the course of this narrative that Pole's instinctive reaction to any proposal of public office was to refuse it. He tried hard, for example, to avoid the Cardinal's hat and he practically refused the Papacy. Hence it is not surprising that Pole shrank from accepting Henry's offer, and in this case his reluctance was increased by his misgivings about the divorce. Misgivings only, it should be noted, not yet a decisive stand against the divorce; he was indeed prepared to accept some sort of a compromise solution. "I remember," he wrote some years later, "saying to Doctor Foxe that I trusted I had found a way to satisfy his Grace. I showed the same to my lord my brother [Lord Montague] and they both informed the King."[13] Henry was naturally very pleased and sent for Reginald. And then the decisive interview took place between these two men.[14]

Reginald was asked to come to York Place, Westminster (Wolsey's old residence, later Whitehall Palace), where he was met by Henry himself at the entrance of a secret gallery. The sudden appearance of the King may have thrown Reginald off his balance. Now there seemed no way out of it, the time had come to explain his plan to the King. But the terms of this carefully considered compromise will for ever remain unknown, because Reginald was unable to put it forward. He was, in fact, tongue-tied. When he recovered his speech, he found himself saying the very opposite of what he had come to say. The King was extremely angry and did not conceal his emotion. He declared that Reginald had greatly offended him, left the room, and banged the door, leaving Reginald in tears. The King was so perturbed that for a while he remained alone in his room.

What subconscious forces caused Reginald's temporary impediment of speech we do not know; he himself, in retrospect, ascribed it to divine intervention. But we might attempt to discuss the factors which must have influenced Reginald's deliberations on this matter. He mentions that members of his family tried to persuade him to accept the divorce. It is unlikely that this refers to his mother, but it may refer to his eldest brother Lord Montague, who probably anticipated the great dangers that would follow Reginald's refusal. And, indeed, Reginald was faced with a genuine dilemma: while his acceptance would be grievous to his mother's dearest friends, the Queen and Princess Mary, his refusal was bound to endanger all members of his family (their final ruin was not long delayed). There is no evidence, on the other hand, that at this stage he was aware of the far-reaching ecclesiastical and political consequences of the divorce. It is well to remember that as late as October 1529 a man of Thomas More's integrity could be persuaded to accept the office of Lord Chancellor, which he did not resign until May 1532, at a time when Pole had already left England.

Among the motives for Reginald's decision was one which he himself repeatedly stressed and to which we must give due weight: his sincere regard for Henry. The King had hitherto shown nothing but kindness and generosity to Reginald, and there seems to have been a genuine mutual affection between the two men. Reginald never attempted to conceal the fact that Henry had supported his prolonged course of studies. Writing to the Emperor Charles V, for instance, he stated: "I loved and venerated the King to whose generosity and care I owe my knowledge of letters."[15] It was just this affection for the King, he maintained, that caused his eventual decision. He claimed to have perceived that the man whom he loved more than anybody else was about to enter the path of dishonour, and he now held it to be his duty to oppose the divorce for the sake of the King's honour and therefore to refuse the Archbishopric of York. "I should have been the greatest enemy of the King," he wrote, "if his honour and salvation had not been dearer to me than any honour he proposed to confer on me."[16] And there is considerable force in this argument. Whatever view posterity may take of the ultimate consequences of the divorce, not even Henry's most ardent apologists will maintain that it ranks among his personally honourable actions. Reginald had every right to show anxiety for the spiritual health of his sovereign.

This was not quite the end of the affair. Reginald was greatly upset by this stormy interview and he tried to find a way to reconcile the King. He decided to send a letter to Henry, carefully explaining his views. When the Duke of Norfolk heard of this letter he complained to Lord Montague that Reginald had committed a fresh outrage against the King. Reginald, however, assured his brother that the letter did not contain anything insulting. Montague thereupon asked for, and was granted, an audience with the King. Henry had completely lost his former anger and told him: "Your brother has explained his reasons with so much affection towards me that I am bound to accept it all in good part." So far everything seemed to go well, but then Henry went on to make an astonishing remark: "And if your brother were now to add his approval of my cause, nobody should be dearer to my heart."[17] This is an interesting example of Henry's almost naïve egotism: he is faced with good reasons against the divorce; he has to respect the sincerity and the good intention of the writer; and yet he seems to expect that the latter will not, after all, draw the obvious conclusion from his arguments and will fall in with the royal design.

Reginald's letter has unfortunately been lost (perhaps it was destroyed by the King), but we know its contents, because Henry asked Thomas Cranmer, who was then rapidly rising in the royal favour, to investigate it. Cranmer's report is extant.[18] Cranmer frankly admitted that if Pole's letter "were set forth and known to the common people, it were not possible to persuade them to the contrary." Pole began by drawing attention to "the trouble, which was like to ensue to this realm by diversity of titles. Whereof what hurt might come, we have had example in our fathers' days by the titles of Lancaster and York." This was just the kind of argument that Henry would have regarded as highly relevant. Henry's claim that the law of God had been violated by his marriage to Katharine, Pole was not prepared to take very seriously. On this point he made the shrewd remark: "As touching the law of God, if the King were pleased to take the contrary part, he might as well justify that." A further argument, which dealt with the international effects of the divorce, deserves honourable mention. Pole rightly emphasized the power of the Emperor Charles V, who happened to be Katharine's nephew, in comparison with France. "The Emperor," he wrote, "may injure us without drawing a sword, by merely forbidding traffic in Flanders and Spain." This sound economic reasoning is noteworthy as coming from a man who is often described as completely ignorant of mundane matters. His firm grasp of the concrete circumstances of the divorce adds strength to Pole's central point: his concern for the King's honour. If he supported the divorce, he explained, he would not only take away the Princess's title, but would have to "accuse the chief part of the King's life hitherto," by having to suppose that Henry had lived for twenty years in a shameful and most unnatural marriage. He concluded by saying that the King "stands on the brink of the water, and yet may save all his honour; but if he put forth his foot but one step forward, all his honour is drowned."

There can be no reasonable doubt that, in addition to his loyalty to Katharine and Mary, his regard for the King's honour went a long way towards helping him to make up his mind. But we must consider yet another motive—one which Pole could not disclose to the King and of which he may not have been clearly aware: his desire to avoid the burdens of a public career and to continue his studies. This may well have been reinforced by a nostalgia for his happy student days on the Continent and by the attractions of a Bembian life of leisure. The time had arrived when he had to forsake the delights of youth and accept the responsibilities of manhood. His up-bringing had allowed him to postpone this transition longer than many other men, but this must have made it all the more difficult for him. He now attempted to evade his destiny by seeking shelter in his past; in order to avoid entering on a new stage of his life, he tried to repeat an old one. And so he asked for Henry's permission to leave England once more and to resume his studies abroad.

Henry seems to have hesitated for a time before giving his consent. Reginald must have written his letter to the King in May or June 1531; he had to wait seven or eight months, until January 1532, before he was allowed to leave the country. The imperial ambassador Chapuys suggested in a dispatch to Charles V that Reginald had made use of a threat: "Pole," he wrote, "told the King that if he remained here he must attend Parliament, and if the divorce were discussed he must speak according to his conscience. On this, the King immediately gave him leave to go."[19] Chapuys may not have got this quite right: it is difficult to see why Pole, who was doing everything in his power to lead a retired life, should have insisted on attending Parliament. Perhaps the ambassador meant Convocation, in which Pole, as Dean of Exeter, had a seat. However that may be, Henry eventually fulfilled Pole's request; he even promised to pay him something like his accustomed annual grant and allowed him to retain his benefices.[20] Thus provided, Reginald left England for the third time. He was not to return for over twenty years.

Reginald had had to face two quite distinct temptations, only one of which he had been able to withstand. The King had offered him power and wealth and he had shown himself free from worldly ambition. But he was more susceptible to the other temptation: that of shirking the worldly duties that happened to come his way. This failing must not be overlooked. Bearing it in mind we shall not be in danger of regarding Pole as a plaster saint. There can be no doubt that Pole's life, seen as a whole, was an exceptionally good one, but even exceptionally good men have to develop and grow; they tend to become completely unintelligible to the common run of us if we forget this simple fact. It was only gradually that Pole learnt to accept the laws of growth and to realize that he could not, without serious harm to himself, re-live his past. It was now required of him that he should become a new man.

NOTES TO CHAPTER TWO

[1] A. F. Pollard, *Henry VIII* (1902), passim.

[2] Castiglione, *The Book of the Courtier*, trans. Sir Thomas Hoby (Everyman's Library), p. 291 (translation slightly altered).

[3] Mountjoy to Erasmus, *Opus Epistolarum Des. Erasmi Roterodami*, ed. Allen, vol. i, No. 215.

[4] Edward Hall, *The Triumphant Reigne of King Henry VIII*, ed. C. Whibley (1904), vol. i, p. 22.

[5] Cf. J. A. Gee, *Life and Works of Thomas Lupset* (1928).

[6] *L. + P.*, vol. iv, No. 6004; vol. v, p. 315.

[7] Pole, *Pro Unitatis Ecclesiasticae Defensione* (1555), fol. 55 b.

[8] *L. + P.*, Addenda, vol. i, No. 689; vol. iv, No. 6252.

[9] *L. + P.*, vol. iv, No. 6383.

[10] *L. + P.*, vol. v, p. 749. On the question of Pole's behaviour, cf. the divergent views of Pastor, Zimmermann, Biron, and Constant.

[11] *L. + P.*, vol. v, App. No. 10.

[12] *Q.*, vol. iv, p. 328.

[13] *L. + P.*, vol. xii, No. 444.

[14] The present account of this interview is based on three descriptions written by Pole himself in 1537 and 1547 (*L. + P.*, vol. xii, No. 444; *Q.*, vol. i, p. 183; *Q.*, vol. iv, p. 330). These versions agree in all essentials, and two of them were addressed to the King's Council, many members of which (e.g. the Duke of Norfolk) would have been able to check any inaccuracies. There is no reason to doubt the substantial truth of the story.

[15] *Q.*, vol. i, p. 67.

[16] *Q.*, vol. i, p. 183.

[17] *Q.*, vol. iv, pp. 331–2.

[18] Strype, *Memorials of Cranmer* (1812), vol. ii, pp. 675–9.

[19] *L. + P.*, vol. v, No. 737.

[20] *L. + P.*, vol. v, No. 737; vol. i, p. 10.

CHAPTER THREE

"VITA ACTIVA"
OR "VITA CONTEMPLATIVA"?
(1532–1535)

POLE'S first destination after leaving England was Avignon, a papal city in the south of France, a well-known seat of learning, and possibly attractive to Pole for its memories of Petrarca. But the climate of Avignon did not suit him, and in October 1532 he went on to Padua where he had felt at home during his student days. Once again he became the centre of a large household; once again he was free to devote himself to learning. But the character of his studies was no longer the same. Cicero and the "litterae humaniores" had faded into the background; now it was theology that occupied his growing mind.

Theology had hitherto not played a conspicuous part in Pole's life. Some rudimentary knowledge of it he may have acquired at Oxford, but neither Leonico nor Bembo would have been able to instruct him in theological matters or even to direct his attention to them. Not one of the friends he had made in Italy had been in any way perturbed by the state of the Church or the religious commotions beyond the Alps. We do not know when Pole decided to take up the study of divinity; from a chance remark in one of his letters it appears that he had become aware of this gap in his education soon after his return to England from Italy.[1] But we get some insight into the workings of his mind at this period from an interesting exchange of letters with Jacopo Sadoleto, the learned bishop of Carpentras near Avignon, whom Pole had visited during his stay in southern France.

Sadoleto, more than twenty years Pole's senior, had been

Bembo's fellow-secretary in the time of Leo X and had, together with Bembo, made the letters emanating from the Papal Curia famous among humanists for their Ciceronian style. Unlike Bembo, however, he outgrew the refined frivolity of these circles. He was among those on whom the apocalyptic Sack of Rome (1527) made an indelible impression; here, he thought, was an event of clearly symbolical significance —God's judgment on Medicean Rome. He withdrew to Carpentras and devoted himself seriously and successfully to his episcopal duties. Like Giberti of Verona, he now belonged to those resident bishops who anticipated the later reforms and by their example helped to bring them about. Sadoleto managed to combine his pastoral efforts with a certain amount of literary work, and just at the time of Pole's visit he had finished a book on education (*De liberis recte instituendis*). He gave Pole a copy of the manuscript, asking him to read it and to hand it on to Bembo. Pole fulfilled these requests, and after his arrival in Italy he felt impelled to write to Sadoleto about this book which was soon to achieve fame as an educational classic. He praised it very much, but he had one very important criticism to make. In Sadoleto's treatise a knowledge of philosophy was described as the highest aim of education. This, Pole suggests, may have been the case in ancient times, when Aristotle, Plato and Cicero were propounding their teachings, but now a new haven is to be aimed at—a much securer and quieter one, shown to us by God Himself. In the light of our new knowledge which surpasses the wisdom of the ancients, philosophy has lost its former function. *Our* guide is theology, the ocean into which all other sciences should flow.[2]

Sadoleto's answer to this vigorous challenge is well considered and substantial. Theology, he writes, is the apex of a building of which philosophy provides the basis and the walls. Without such foundations a science of theology cannot be sustained, and this, he rightly adds, was the common conviction of all the Fathers of the Church. Further, great care has to be taken in deciding what kind of theology is worth studying. One can safely follow the Fathers (Chrysostom in particular), but one must beware of the scholastics who wrote such voluminous, unshapely books in a quarrelsome spirit.[3] Pole's answer, if he ever wrote one, is not extant, but he would no doubt have made it clear that he did not hold a brief for the scholastics; even in later life he disregarded all scholastic theology, sometimes to a dangerous extent. What he did wish to do, however, was to restore the balance by a revival of religious studies which had been almost entirely neglected by his circle of friends, and in this respect Sadoleto followed his example. Just then Sadoleto had been hesitating for some time whether he should continue an earlier philosophical treatise of his or turn to a commentary on the Epistle to the Romans. Bembo, whom he had asked for advice, had characteristically urged him to write on philosophy, but under Pole's influence he now decided to devote himself to the Pauline commentary.

Meanwhile Pole had resumed his studies in Padua, paying frequent visits to Venice. At first he had hoped to devote some of his time to humanist subjects and for this reason he had taken into his house the Professor of Rhetoric at Padua, the then famous Lazaro Bonamico. But soon he came to the conclusion that theology "does not easily admit the company of other interests"; he hardly dared to turn his eyes "towards the more elegant studies." As a consequence he found that, contrary to his expectations, he had nothing to say to his prominent guest, a man whose company he would have highly valued in his student days. He now poured scorn on the studies which he himself had so zealously pursued only a few years before: did not all Bonamico's learning lead merely to a mastery of disciplines that were suitable for schoolboys? should not the knowledge of classical authors be applied to higher ends?[4] It does not appear that the accomplished Italian scholar was in any way influenced by Pole's change of mind; he remained what he had always been—an elegant Renaissance professor of elegant letters.

The other inhabitants of Pole's house in Padua formed a

miscellaneous group of scholars and servants. In some cases, indeed, it was not quite clear whether a particular member of his household was to be regarded as a scholar or a servant. A certain Bernardino Sandro, for example, was primarily a valet and house steward, but he was also expected to copy and collate Latin and Greek manuscripts. George Lily, on the other hand, was the son of the first headmaster of St. Paul's School and certainly a scholar, but he complained that he did not get enough time for study in Pole's house. In Padua he had to accompany his master out of doors, according to the prevailing custom, and he found that very wearying. In Venice a hired gondoliere relieved him of this irksome duty, and he therefore welcomed Pole's visits to the metropolis. Not so Bernardino. Nobody, according to an old saying, is regarded as a hero by his valet, and Pole was no exception. Bernardino strongly disapproved of Pole's nomadic habits and his innumerable friendships. Some of his friends came in for Bernardino's special wrath, for dragging "il Signore" from one place to another and for using his house as if it were their own. "We are all tired of this way of living," the valet grumbled. "It is expensive enough to keep house here but much more to move about. Some ill may come of it, at least to us poor servants."[5]

All we can derive from these men is incidental information about Pole's outward life, but from one member of that household we can gather something about Pole's inward development in the first two years (1532–34) of what became his long period of exile. This is Thomas Starkey, who had been a contemporary of Pole's at Oxford and afterwards Fellow of Magdalen College and lecturer in natural philosophy. It seems that Starkey was reading law during his stay in Padua and so would not have shared Pole's actual studies, but Pole in this new phase of his life was likely to find the serious-minded Starkey more congenial than most of his Italian companions; it may be assumed that the two old friends would have had many conversations together. We happen to be in possession of a highly interesting treatise from Starkey's pen, written

between 1533 and 1535 and purporting to be an account of a
dialogue between Pole and Thomas Lupset while both of them
were in England.[6] It is quite possible that these two men
actually had such a conversation before 1530, the year of Lupset's
death, or that Starkey's work is mainly based on his own earlier
acquaintance with Pole, but his membership of Pole's household
in Italy must have done much to increase his familiarity with
his high-born friend. Starkey's treatise deals with problems of
political science, particularly the nature of a true commonwealth and the chief social evils of contemporary England.
Though Pole is the main speaker throughout, Lupset merely
putting forward objections which are generally refuted, we
cannot be quite certain that every one of Pole's alleged opinions
was actually held by him at that time. In most cases, however,
there seems to be no reason why Starkey should have distorted
Pole's views. We can, at any rate, regard this work as evidence
that questions of this kind were discussed in Pole's circle.

This is all the more plausible as the dialogue opens with a
discussion of a problem that must have been uppermost in
Pole's mind: whether it was his duty to enter public life instead
of devoting himself to his studies. The old school problem of
"vita activa" versus "vita contemplativa" was thus experienced by Pole in an acutely personal way, for "vita activa,"
in his case, seemed to imply his participation in English politics,
in a secular or ecclesiastical capacity. Should he, perhaps,
have accepted Henry's offer? Here is what Lupset, in Starkey's
treatise, is made to say on this point, and these words must
have found a lively echo in Pole's mind: "I have much and
many times marvelled, reasoning with myself, why you, Master
Pole, after so many years spent in quiet studies of letters and
learning, and after such experience of the manners of man,
taken in divers parts beyond the sea, have not before this
settled yourself and applied your mind to the handling of the
matters of the common weal here in our own nation. . . .
Me seemeth, whosoever he be which, drawn by the sweetness of
his studies, and by his own quietness and pleasure moved,

leaves the cure of the common weal and policy, he does manifest wrong to his country and friends. . . . Of this, Master Pole, many men do you accuse, saying that, since you have been of your country so well nourished and brought up, you ought now to study to maintain and advance the weal of this same your country."[7] Pole meets this forceful attack by admitting that he is not at all sure whether perfection lies in active or contemplative life. Lupset answers that perfection no doubt includes the practice of contemplation and the knowledge of philosophy, but that another part of it consists in trying to improve others, and this can only be done in the course of an active life. Pole grants the force of this argument but adds repeatedly that the time and place of such an active interference in worldly matters must be well considered; when tyranny and selfishness prevail, "vita activa" cannot be recommended.

Tyranny and Selfishness: these are the roots of the social evils which Pole and Lupset discuss throughout the book. In view of the fact that Henry VIII was meant to read this treatise and was indeed presented with a copy of it, it is particularly remarkable how vigorously it condemns royal absolutism. "This has been thought," runs a typical passage, "yea, and this yet is thought to pertain to the majesty of a prince—to moderate and rule all things according to his will and pleasure; which is, without doubt and ever has been, the greatest destruction to this realm." And again: to leave everything "to the free will and liberty of one is the open gate to all tyranny. This is the ground of the destruction of all civility."[8] It may be doubted whether these reformers would have been so strongly aware of this danger had not Pole, a few years before, received a particularly shocking lesson in the theory of modern absolutism from no less eminent a political practitioner than Thomas Cromwell. Together with Pole's earlier diplomatic experiences during his friendship with Pace, this conversation with Cromwell must have done much to increase his insight into contemporary politics.

This famous interview, like the decisive encounter between

Pole and Henry, took place in Cardinal Wolsey's palace in Westminster, at a time when Cromwell was still in Wolsey's service (in 1527 or 1528). Pole had only just returned from Italy, and Cromwell, probably in order to find out which side Pole would take in the divorce controversy, asked him what, in his view, were the duties of a good statesman. Pole innocently suggested that the statesman should, above all, have his sovereign's honour at heart. This answer seems to have amused Cromwell, and he proceeded to ridicule it. He had no doubt that such a statement sounded very attractive and that it would be sure of praise at an academic disputation. But in the secret councils of state it was not of much use. There, it would be regarded as insipid and, so far from gaining applause, would be violently rejected and would lead to ruin. For considerations of honour rarely coincided with the Prince's will, and it was a statesman's chief duty to find out in which direction the Prince's will was tending. This, of course, was not the kind of thing one was likely to learn in universities! It was a very difficult task requiring much experience and unusual prudence, because the Prince's words did not always indicate his desires. In his public pronouncements he had to use the high-sounding phrases about religion, piety, and all the other virtues, but his real wishes might be very different. The good statesman, therefore, had to take pains to discover what the Prince wished to achieve, and then to help him to achieve it without any loss of public reputation.

It may be supposed that such talk was common enough among courtiers. But at this point of the conversation something very interesting happened. Cromwell concluded his political lecture to the young royal kinsman with a reference to an authority on the subject. True, the writer whose work he was about to mention was not one of the ancient authors, he was in fact a contemporary, but an extremely ingenious and acute thinker, who, instead of pursuing his dreams, had described what was borne out by everyday political experience. This writer, it seems, was Machiavelli,[9] and Cromwell promised to send Pole a copy of the book in which these views were expounded. He actually did not keep his promise, but Pole obtained a copy later on and studied Machiavelli's teaching. His verdict was terse: "I found that this book had been written by an enemy of the human race." Much has since been said in Machiavelli's defence, but whatever his ultimate convictions may have been, he did, in his *Principe*, furnish a theoretical justification for what statesmen like Cromwell were doing at that time. Pole must have felt that something entirely new was happening under his very eyes. He must have known how often politicians did not practise what they preached, but here their most evil practices were being coolly and shamelessly recommended. The fateful divorce of politics and ethics had begun.

This contemporary conflict adds force and interest to Pole's developed political views. They were, of course, nourished and shaped by his fundamental ethical convictions; behind them was the time-honoured, hallowed tradition of Christian humanism, based on the conception of divinely inspired reason ("recta ratio"). "The goodness of God," Pole declares in Starkey's *Dialogue*, ". . . has made man, of all creatures in earth, most perfect, giving unto him a sparkle of his own divinity—that is to say, right reason—whereby he should govern himself in civil life and good policy, according to his excellent nature and divinity."[10] But in addition to this spark of divine reason, man also contains passions and vicious desires, and if he submits to them he is no more than a brute beast. This applies equally to whole nations. A nation can be ruled by good laws and so echo the divine harmony prevailing in the universe; or one man, given to brutish desires, can disturb the harmony and establish his tyrannical rule, and then "hark! what discord follows." Tyranny is doubtless only one of the possible perversions of the "good society," but Pole evidently felt that it was this perversion, rather than any other, that was endangering the social order in his time.

From certain passages in the *Dialogue* it emerges how

strongly Pole was influenced by the example of the Venetian constitution, which he had been able to study as a young man; in the course of his life he came to regard Venice as his second home.[11] Venice "once held the gorgeous East in fee," but now she no longer exists as a separate state and we tend to forget with what awe her constitution was regarded at the time of her greatness. Pole praised "the most noble city of Venice, which, by the reason of the good order and policy that therein is used, has continued about a thousand years in one order and state,"[12] and this sentiment was shared by many of his contemporaries. The Venetian constitution, to be sure, was based on an extremely complicated system of checks and counter-checks and in this form was incapable of imitation elsewhere. But its importance to the sixteenth-century political theorist lay in the fact that it resulted in a mixed government, and that the headship of the state was elective and not hereditary. In Castiglione's *Cortegiano*, for example, Bembo, a native of Venice, is made to describe with great pride the unique Venetian balance between republican liberty and a strong monarchical government. It is this Venetian self-confidence that appears in his well-known contribution to the discussion on the best state (and it is more than likely that Pole would have heard these views from Bembo himself): "Since God has given liberty for a sovereign gift, it is not reason that it should be taken from us: nor that one man should be partner of it more than another, which happens under the rule of Princes, who for the most part keep their people in most strait bondage. But in common weals well in order this liberty is well kept."[13]

Something of this spirit informs Pole's views on the safeguards against that outstanding political evil, tyranny. Royal power, he thought, should not be based on hereditary succession but on election. The King should be elected by Parliament, which should be assembled only for this purpose "or else for some other great urgent course concerning the common state and policy." At all other times the authority of Parliament was to be vested in a council consisting of four peers, two bishops (London and Canterbury), four of the chief judges, and four citizens of London. In case of any royal attempt at tyranny this Council was to summon Parliament and to bring about a "reformation" of the whole state of the commonalty. Whether in such an emergency Parliament can depose the King is not directly discussed, but this can be deduced from the general statement that tyrants should be deposed.[14]

In Starkey's *Dialogue* there are references to a large variety of contemporary social evils, and these passages have naturally aroused more interest among historians than any other part of the book, but it should be stressed that the condemnation of these evils is inseparably connected with the fundamental ideas of the treatise as a whole. There were only few men, so its chief complaint could be summed up, who had the interests of the community at heart; most people, under the pretence of serving the public good, really pursued "the private and the singular weal."[15] This can justly be regarded as an echo of More's famous indictment in *Utopia*, but it is more than that as well, because More's stricture, in its turn, refers back to traditional social thought. "We are members one of another" (Eph. iv, 25): it was this conviction that was always implied. We still speak of the "body politic," but we tend to forget the profound meaning of this metaphor. Pole, like so many before him, thought of society as a body and therefore of the various social classes as parts of the body, the ruler corresponding to the heart, the ruler's officers to the head, the eyes and the ears, the craftsmen and soldiers to the hands, and the peasants to the feet. Social health and strength depends on constant co-operation of all members of society in the interest of the whole, every one doing his duty "with brotherly love." Moreover, in addition to health and strength, beauty must be aimed at by a civilized society, and beauty results from the due proportion of all the parts, "so that one part ever be agreeable to another in form and fashion, quantity and number."[16] (It is interesting to see how easily the Hellenic idea

41

of proportion and beauty, revived by the Renaissance, could combine with the Christian teaching of membership in the body of Christ.)

Starting from such conceptions of a healthy and beautiful social organism, Pole was able to diagnose many social ills and deformities, fancifully identifying them with such physical diseases as frenzy, dropsy, or gout. Two of the most prominent ills, he thought, were a general decline in the numbers of the English population and a high degree of poverty. This is not the place for a discussion of these statements in the light of modern research; with the first of them many social historians would be inclined to agree,[17] while they would probably deny the second. Here it is intended to use them merely as evidence for the lively interest in these matters on the part of Pole and some of his friends. The careful consideration of these points in Starkey's treatise clearly shows that this interest was intelligent and well informed. Lupset, while accepting the decline of population in England as a fact, advances the view that the agriculture of the country cannot support more people. Pole retorts that the land, well occupied and tilled, can feed a larger population; the prevailing poverty is not due to natural causes. Then Lupset expresses his doubts about this alleged poverty; is not England, at any rate, richer than France, Italy, or Spain? Pole agrees (this is interesting in itself in view of his knowledge of the Continent), but he sticks to his view that England is now poorer than in the past. Lupset remains unconvinced and this point is left undecided. Both of them agree, however, that the wealth of England, whatever its absolute size, is badly distributed—"some have too much, some too little, and some never a whit."[18] Such lack of "due proportion" can also be discovered in the occupations of the English people: there are too many idle hangers-on of the nobility; the prelates and the monks are ill-occupied; and there are too many who "busy themselves in making and procuring things for the vain pastime and pleasure of others."[19] These luxuries are eagerly sought after by the rich, who, on the other hand, neglect their duties towards the poor, only looking to "the receiving of their rents and revenues of their lands, with great study of enhancing thereof, to the further maintaining of their pompous state."[20] This results in a general rise in prices and in much poverty among the lower classes. Lupset suggests that the enclosure of arable land for pasture is among the causes of poverty, but Pole, unlike some other contemporary observers including More, refuses to condemn this practice outright, as cattle and wool are indispensable to the prosperity of the country. Once again agreement is reached by applying the criterion of "due proportion." Care must be taken that there should not be too much pasture-land as compared with arable, and that the pasture-land should not get into the hands of a few rich men, to the detriment of the poor. The agrarian history of the sixteenth century provides a sad commentary on this protest against social injustice.

These, then, are some of the subjects which were probably discussed by Starkey and Pole when they were living together in Padua. Starkey seems to have had some political ambitions and may well have considered it his duty to draw his friend's attention to these problems, in the hope of persuading him to devote himself to politics. At the same time, it must be remembered that Starkey was a priest; as such he cannot have been entirely unaware of Pole's new interests. It is therefore not surprising that a discussion of certain ecclesiastical matters is also included in the *Dialogue*. From these passages Pole emerges as a radical Church reformer, and this is, in fact, what he was about to become. But here, more than anywhere else, it is difficult to distinguish between Starkey's own views and those ascribed to Pole. It is uncertain, for example, whether Pole would have actually referred to the monks as "idle abbey-lubbers, which are apt to nothing but only to eat and drink,"[21] though Pole is not made to demand their suppression but merely a thoroughgoing monastic reform. Still, on this point, Starkey, who came to approve Henry's dissolution of the monasteries, may have given expression to his own bias.

But there is no reason to doubt that Pole really held some of the other ecclesiastical views ascribed to him. He is made to attack the unlimited dispensing power of the Pope "the which by money his officers do sell"; to complain that cardinals' hats are frequently sold or bestowed on unworthy persons; and to assert that most priests "can nothing do but patter up their matins and mass," mumbling a certain number of words which they do not understand. "The magnificence and majesty of the Church," is his summary, "stands not in possessions and pomp, but in stableness and purity of Christian life."[22]

"The purity of Christian life": this was indeed the essence of the sorely needed reform, and here, Pole insists, the priests and other dignitaries must set the example. On this point he uses the parallel of the "good society": "As the restoring of the civil life stands chiefly in heads and rulers, . . . in so much that if this be good, all the communalty will follow the same, so the confirming and stabling of this celestial doctrine stands chiefly in the officers thereof; that is to say, in the preachers, in the godly living and doctrine of them."[23] Residence of all pastors must be strictly insisted on, and just as "by order of law the poor men are bounden to pay their tithes to their curate, so likewise they which are parsons and curates should be bounden to distribute that which they have superfluous among the poverty of their parish." A bishop, for the same reason, should divide his possessions into four parts: the first to build and repair churches; the second to support poor scholars; the third for other needy persons in his care; and only the fourth to provide for himself and his household.[24]

Starkey, we may conclude, knew and shared Pole's concern for Church reform, but, despite his international contacts, he remained thoroughly insular and continued to think of these matters in terms of England alone. He was evidently convinced (and this conviction may have been quite genuine) that Henry VIII could be made to see the excellence of all these reform proposals and, having done so, would bring them about. Starkey left Pole towards the end of 1534 and returned to

England where he became one of the King's chaplains. It was at this stage that he presented his remarkable treatise to the King. One of the first tasks that Henry asked him to perform was to persuade his old friend Pole to change his mind about the divorce and to return to England. Starkey accepted this task and seems to have been confident that Pole would give up his earlier opposition.

Starkey's expectation, it so happens, turned out to be quite wrong. What was actually going on in Pole's mind was more accurately hinted at by an otherwise unknown acquaintance of his who reported in 1535: "Pole is studying divinity and talking of high things, despising things merely human and terrestrial. O wondrous transformation through which he exchanges man for God!"[25] It was this transformation that enabled Pole for the first time to grasp the fundamental conflict of his life. The possibility of "vita activa" in the service of his royal cousin had been constantly before him since his student days, but the humanist alternative to it was a "vita contemplativa" only in name, not in substance. Now, for the first time, the religious life presented itself as an alternative: a life of prayer and meditation, and of study of the Holy Scriptures. It was now (some time in 1535) that he met the well-known biblical scholar Joannes Campensis and read with him Isaiah, beside whose words the eloquence of Cicero and the pictorial richness of Homer paled into insignificance.[26] Now he also gained the friendship of some very distinguished and devout men who, for one reason or another, were at that time in or near Venice. In October 1535 Pole moved to Venice and lived in a house on the Grand Canal ("between the house of Foscari and the ferry of St. Barnabas"). We catch various glimpses of Pole, engaged in intimate and intense conversations with his new friends. The most vivid of these scenes we owe to the writer Antonio Bruccioli who, in one of his Dialogues, describes a visit to the celebrated monastery of S. Giorgio Maggiore in Venice: "Tempted by the pleasant season, the early hour, and the beauty of the spot I asked the brothers to open the door of their most lovely garden; and one of them having done so, while the singing of the birds filled the heavens, I perceived il Signore Rinaldo [Pole] at the entrance of the little wood in earnest talk with Theogono, bidding him follow virtue with all his strength."[27] Pole himself tells us that, walking in the gardens of the Benedictine estate of Rovelone near Mantua together with two of his friends, it seemed to him that he was "walking with Enoch and Elias in God's Paradise." Another of his letters from Rovelone ends in a similar vein: "Farewell. From our Paradise: for such, in truth, may I call this place where I now reside, both on account of the pleasant country and most delightful hills, and yet more by reason of the companions whose society I enjoy here . . . I hear nothing but the praise of God; and in this delicious spot I fancy myself with my maker in Paradise."[28]

The men whose life Pole came to share in an ever increasing degree were ecclesiastical dignitaries, monks, and laymen, whose common concern was the reform of the Church. One of the most prominent members of this group was the learned Abbot of San Giorgio Maggiore, Gregorio Cortese. Another monk, known to us simply by his Christian name Mark, seems to have had a considerable influence on Pole by his expositions of the Scriptures; he was, according to Pole's first biographer, a man who combined the highest scholarship with the highest devotion.[29] Then there was the Venetian nobleman Alvise Priuli, a lovable and high-minded man, Pole's life-long friend and faithful to him to the last. (During these years Pole spent much time in Priuli's country house near Treviso.) But we still have to mention the two men for whose sake in particular Pole felt himself drawn to Venice: Bishop Gian Pietro Caraffa, the founder of the Theatines and future Pope, and the Venetian senator Gasparo Contarini. For Caraffa Pole had unbounded admiration ("vir sanctissimus et doctissimus," he called him,[30]) but Contarini he soon came to love more than any other of his many friends, and Contarini found in the gentle Englishman a kindred spirit whose experiences had prepared him for the great work that was about to come to fruition. It was to Contarini, more than to anybody else, that Pole owed the final solution of his prolonged personal conflict. Having speculated much on the requirements and problems of a good life, he now realized that it was possible to live a "vita activa" in the service of a contemplative ideal.

NOTES TO CHAPTER THREE

[1] *Q.*, vol. i. p. 401.

[2] *Q.*, vol. i, pp. 399–401.

[3] *Q.*, vol. i, pp. 405–21.

[4] *Q.*, vol. i, pp. 410–12.

[5] *L. + P.*, vol. ix, Nos. 512, 673. For Sandro's copying efforts, cf. E. Lobel, "Cardinal Pole's MSS." (*Proceedings of the British Academy*, 1931).

[6] *England in the Reign of King Henry the Eighth*, part 2, ed. J. M. Cowper (Early English Text Society, 1871), henceforth referred to as *Dialogue* (I have modernized the spelling). It is now easily accessible in a new edition by K. M. Burton (1948). For the date of the treatise, cf. Miss Burton's discussion, op. cit., pp. 193–6.

[7] *Dialogue*, pp. 2–3.

[8] *Dialogue*, pp. 101, 103.

[9] The only extant account of it is given by Pole himself in his *Apologia ad Carolum Quintum Caesarem*, written in 1538 or 1539 (*Q.*, vol. i, pp. 133 seq.). P. van Dyke (*American Historical Review*, 1904, pp. 712 seq.) suggests that the book mentioned by Cromwell was Castiglione's *Cortegiano*, not Machiavelli's *Principe*, but I do not find his arguments convincing.

[10] *Dialogue*, p. 165.

[11] *S.P. Ven.*, vol. vi, part 2, No. 884.

[12] *Dialogue*, p. 179.

[13] Castiglione, *The Book of the Courtier*, transl. Hoby (Everyman's Library), p. 274.

[14] *Dialogue*, pp. 167, 169, 170, 182.

[15] *Dialogue*, p. 85.

[16] *Dialogue*, pp. 49, 51.

[17] Cf. John Saltmarsh's important article "Plague and Economic Decline in England in the later Middle Ages" (*Cambridge Historical Journal*, 1941), where a serious decline of the population in the fifteenth century is suggested.

[18] *Dialogue*, p. 92.

[19] *Dialogue*, p. 80.

[20] *Dialogue*, p. 85.

[21] *Dialogue*, p. 131. Similarly, it may be doubted whether Starkey's strong opposition to clerical celibacy represents a view held by Pole then or at any other time.

[22] *Dialogue*, pp. 123, 124, 126, 132.
[23] *Dialogue*, p. 209.
[24] *Dialogue*, pp. 200–1.
[25] *L. + P.*, vol. ix, No. 917 (translation altered).
[26] F. Dittrich, *Kardinal Contarini* (1885), p. 217.
[27] Bruccioli's description is quoted in *Q.*, vol. i, pp. 301–2. I follow the translation given in M. Haile, *Life of Reginald Pole* (1910), p. 128. For the location of Pole's house in Venice, cf. *L. + P.*, vol. ix, No. 659.
[28] *Q.*, vol. i, p. 475; *S.P. Ven.*, vol. v, No. 116.
[29] *Q.*, vol. i, p. 11.
[30] *Q.*, vol. i., p. 417.

CHAPTER FOUR

THE DECISION
(1535–1536)

I. *Catholic Reform*

POLE was immensely fortunate in gaining Contarini's friendship at the very time when he needed it most. Gasparo Contarini, who was nearly twenty years older than Pole, could look back on an interesting and successful life, rich in thought as well as in action. He was a member of one of the oldest aristocratic families in Venice, and as such he occupied a natural place in the political life of his native city. But before he entered on this predestined career he followed the equally natural course of studying at the Venetian university of Padua (1501–9). There he was exposed to substantially the same influences as Pole was to encounter twenty years later: enthusiastic study of the classical languages and of Greek philosophy. He was taught philosophy by Padua's greatest light, Pietro Pomponazzi, and he also acquired an intimate knowledge of Homer, Virgil, Horace, Lucretius, and Cicero. We have it on his own authority that in his days, too, theological studies were neglected at Padua,[1] but he himself was not guilty of such a neglect. He seems to have taken a regular course in theology; his writings, even his earliest, show that he knew the Fathers and among the later doctors particularly St. Thomas Aquinas. His first literary attempt was a book on the immortality of the soul, in which he tried to show, in opposition to the teaching of Pomponazzi, that this doctrine can be established by natural reason. Pomponazzi, whose real beliefs and intentions are difficult to know, had countered earlier objections against his views by explaining that he had merely asserted the inability

E   49

of natural reason to apprehend the immortality of the soul; the doctrine itself, he held, must be believed on the authority of the Christian Church. Such a dichotomy between reason and faith was unacceptable to Contarini.[2] He was firmly convinced that the reasoning power of man could be freed from its imperfections by Revelation without any resulting strain from paradoxes and antinomies. We can perhaps say that he was attempting to regain the great synthesis of reason and faith achieved by St. Thomas Aquinas over two centuries earlier— an intellectual synthesis eminently congenial to his predisposition for spiritual harmony.

He continued to devote some time to academic studies in the course of his life, but mainly in the intervals of his public career. After his return from the University he took his place on the Great Council of Venice. In 1521 his fellow citizens showed their appreciation of his work and character by appointing him ambassador to the Emperor Charles V. During this embassy, which lasted until 1525 and took him to Germany, the Netherlands and Spain, he must have acquired much political experience. He also found time to write an interesting and influential political treatise, *De Magistratibus et republica Venetorum*. After little over two years' rest he was honoured with an equally important task: he was made Venetian ambassador to Pope Clement VII. In this capacity he was able to obtain much insight into the character of that vacillating Pope and the general conditions of the Papal Curia during the years immediately following the sack of Rome. He returned to Venice in 1530 and, in addition to filling various high posts in the Venetian administration, he became a member of the group of Church reformers that had gathered round Cortese and Caraffa. Though only a layman himself, he seems to have impressed his fellow members by the purity of his life, the rare distinction of his mind, and his wide experience. Throughout his life he was thus able to grow quietly and naturally; to develop, in Ranke's unforgettable words, "like a tree, adding ring to ring in regular sequence."[3] Here, then, was a man with a background very similar to Pole's, who had been able to avoid or to solve the painful conflicts of Pole's life: a humanist but a theologian too, and evidently capable of combining action with genuine contemplation. He alone among the members of that Venetian circle was in quite that position, and this is why he could help Pole so decisively. No other member of this circle, it should be added, perhaps no other Italian of that time, was so truly akin to Thomas More.

The kind of contribution that this great Venetian was likely to make to the cause of Church reform can easily be deduced from his character. He was a man of high ideals, and though he was not by nature given to radical courses of action, his embassy to the Curia seems to have convinced him that nothing but a radical cure would have any effect at all. For a long time Church reform had been on the agenda, but so far without avail. His penetrating mind enabled him to go to the real roots of the disease that had befallen the Church of Christ. In the course of an exciting conversation with Pope Clement VII he stated parts of his searching diagnosis with astonishing force.[4] The diplomatic background of this interview does not concern us here. Contarini's immediate intention was to gain the Pope's allegiance to the Imperial League, but in order to achieve this limited purpose he used arguments of far wider importance. He was alone with the Pope and made it clear that he would speak, not as an ambassador, but as a private individual and a Christian. "I can see," he began to explain, "that your Holiness has certain interests as the ruler of a temporal state and is about to take one of two courses of action: either to prefer these particular interests to the common good, or to aim principally at the common good of Christendom and at universal peace, allowing the particular interests to fall into the background." To take the second course, he added, was indispensable for the establishment of universal peace. The Pope's cautious reply that in his secular policy he was not pursuing his particular interests but those of the Church, drew an impassioned reply from Contarini: "Your

Holiness should not suppose," he said, "that the well-being of the Church of Christ is bound up with this little temporal state. Before ever such a state existed, there was a Church, and indeed the Church was then in her best condition. The Church is the community of all Christians. The Papal state is simply the state of an Italian prince joined to the Church." The Pope's answer to this unanswerable statement was remarkable. He began by admitting that Contarini had spoken the truth. But then he went on to put forward the perennial excuse of the "Realpolitiker": his opponents were not animated by ideal motives and he had to play their game. "Nowadays," he told Contarini, "the world has been reduced to such a state that the astutest and craftiest man gains most applause and fame, while if one acts otherwise one is simply considered a good-natured but worthless fellow." This statement by the Head of the Christian Church affords us a valuable insight into the insidious effects of a secularization that was no longer noticed. Had Pope Clement, one is tempted to ask, never pondered 1 Cor. iii 19: "The wisdom of this world is foolishness with God"? Did he not remember that the world had ever preferred Barabbas to Christ, and that Barabbas was a robber? Even if he knew all this, he was unwilling to apply it to the conduct of public affairs. In view of Clement's spiritual blindness Contarini's reply to him was unlikely to meet with an adequate response: "If your Holiness were to consider all the contents of Holy Scripture, which cannot err, he would see that nothing is stronger and more vigorous than truth, virtue, goodness, and a right intention. In many individual cases I have tested this and found it true."

Clement VII remained uninfluenced by Contarini's arguments. As long as he continued to wear the tiara there was no hope for any reform, let alone a radical one. During that period of Papal history the personal qualities of a Pope counted for more than anything else. The Conciliar Movement of the fifteenth century had failed to provide a constitutional basis for the Church, and the worldly Renaissance Popes were making good use of the contemporary tendency towards absolute monarchy—absolute in relation not only to constitutional control but to the moral law itself. There were some canonists who exalted the papal "plenitudo potestatis" to such an extent that in their teaching the Pope's will tended to become the sole criterion of law. Just as Pole opposed the parallel current of secular political thought, represented by Machiavelli and Cromwell, so Contarini explicitly attacked this theory of papal absolutism. Papal rule, he holds, like any other form of authority, must be rational, because it is exercised over rational beings. To ascribe unlimited power to the Pope amounts to idolatry. Such a doctrine is also incompatible with the law of Christ, which is the law of freedom. Subjection to the arbitrary will of a ruler, instead of common obedience to natural law, is nothing but slavery and captivity. And Contarini goes so far as to suggest that the pernicious errors on this point explain the appearance of such protests as Luther's "Babylonian Captivity of the Church."[5]

This reference to Lutheranism could be misunderstood. It might appear to justify the view that the Catholic reform movement was merely a belated response to the Protestant challenge (the well-established term "Counter-Reformation" implies such an opinion). This, however, is not the whole truth. Though Contarini was greatly perturbed by the Protestant secession and devoted much energy, during the remaining years of his life, to attempts at bridging the widening gulf, his zeal for Church reform went back to a time before the beginning of Luther's public career.

As early as 1516 Contarini wrote a book, which was to make him famous in reform circles, on the duties of a bishop (*De officio episcopi libri duo*). Writing at a time when Machiavelli and Castiglione were laying down new-fangled rules for princes and courtiers, he expounded deliberately old-fashioned rules for bishops. A bishop's prime duty, he taught, is to embody all the virtues. How else can he, as he is clearly expected to, lead his fellow Christians to the highest beatitude? It is he who will make or mar the Christian community that is entrusted to his care, just as the civil ruler is ultimately responsible for the state of the body politic. Some virtues, such as justice, temperance, fortitude, apply equally to a civil and a spiritual ruler. Similarly, learning and a certain urbanity of manners are necessary to both of them. But the bishop must, in addition, cultivate the three theological virtues faith, hope, and charity, and especially the last, for without it even his most honest and righteous actions would be comparable to a beautiful yet lifeless marble statue. Various acts of charity which fall within a bishop's province are then outlined and recommended. On the other hand, any expenditure for purposes of ostentation are severely censured. "Nothing," Contarini writes, "is more unbecoming to a pastor of a Christian flock than such outward pomp as grand dinners, a huge crowd of servants, a large and exquisite collection of tapestries and silver vessels, not to mention the more disgraceful expenses."[6]

Contarini would have been the first to admit that his eloquent description of a good bishop was bound to remain as lifeless as a marble statue if it was not brought to life by real bishops. Fortunately it was brought to life just then, and most influentially, by a personal friend of Contarini's, Gian Matteo Giberti, Bishop of Verona, the bishop *par excellence* of the Catholic reform.[7] Like Contarini, Giberti started his public career as a politician. As a young man of eighteen (he was born in 1495) he entered the service of Cardinal Medici, the future Pope Clement VII. Even under Leo X he was often entrusted with important tasks, but he rose to the highest rank when his master succeeded to the Papacy in 1523. Giberti became in effect Clement's Prime Minister. By this time Giberti had developed great religious zeal and would have preferred spiritual work, but he found it impossible to refuse the wish of his old master and patron, whose captivity he shared during the sack of Rome. After this catastrophe, however, he decided to devote himself to the work of his diocese Verona.

He began his task in the way which Contarini had suggested:

54

by altering his own life. He resigned all his other benefices to which a cure of souls was attached, and he modelled his household on a semi-monastic pattern. "There were stated times for divine service, for giving audience, for meals, for social intercourse and literary labours. Seven hours at most was all he allowed himself for repose. He rose early and devoted the early morning hours to religious exercises. He gave audience to suitors both before and after the morning mass, always receiving the poor, and especially those who came from the country, first. All day long he busied himself with the cares of his diocese and the superintendence of the work of editing the rare treasures of his library. In the evening he once more gave audience, and ended the day with a recitation of the penitential psalms with his household."[8]

Having put his own house in order, he could proceed to clean up his diocese. As almost everywhere, abuses were rampant in the ecclesiastical life of Verona. "Many of the clergy were non-resident, leaving the cure of souls to hirelings who, for the most part, were persons of demoralized habits. The ignorance of many of them was so great that Giberti had to order the rubrics of the Missal to be translated into Italian for the sake of those who knew no Latin. Preaching in many places had been given up altogether. The confessional was treated with laxity, and the churches were so neglected that they looked like stables."[9] Giberti's first step in his reform work was a searching visitation of his diocese. Non-resident and immoral priests were dismissed, without regard to their patrons; all dispensations for holding a plurality of benefices were revoked; parish priests were forced to fulfil their preaching duties and to see to the dignity of the worship; overseers were appointed to control the execution of these and all other visitation orders.

Next came the monasteries and nunneries. Their state was appalling, and some of them offered a spirited opposition to any attempts at reform. Some nuns, most of them daughters of the Veronese nobility, held out against their bishop for many

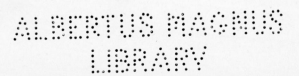

years, but eventually Giberti got his way in every case by his energy and pertinacity. Some convents of particularly evil repute he closed altogether and never relaxed his watch over the others. This strict régime which, it must be added in fairness to Clement VII, was fully backed up by the powers of the Papacy, was bound to be successful in the end. Giberti's forceful example, together with that of men like Sadoleto, did much to raise the moral prestige of the Church in the days before the Council of Trent.[10]

Giberti's expenditure of the episcopal revenue followed the lines laid down by the reformers. Most of it was used for a variety of charitable purposes. The ravages of invasion and war had caused much acute poverty and distress, which the Bishop resolutely set out to remedy. He adopted the distinction that was to underlie the Elizabethan Poor Law, between "sturdy beggars" who were set to work in workhouses and those who were willing but unable to work. The latter were provided with money, clothes and medical help. In addition, Giberti founded orphanages, a hospital for aliens, and a home for reformed prostitutes. For the administration of this comprehensive poor law system he established a special fraternity called the Society of Charity. The aim of this society, in the words of a contemporary, was "that no man should suffer hunger, no man do injury to his neighbour, no man, above all things, commit sin, no man be deprived of the necessities of life; finally, that enmity and all hatred and anger should be taken away, so that we, as men once did in the first and happiest days of the Church, should all live with one heart and one soul in the fear and praise of God."[11]

The life of a man so fully and productively occupied by the kind of work he liked best must surely be called happy. There is nothing to suggest that Giberti ever missed the refined comforts of the Papal Curia he had now left for good. His leisure hours in Verona were devoted to scholarship and the society of learned friends. Giberti was less of a theologian than Contarini, but he took part in the Erasmian attempt to lay bare the springs of Christian theology. He had collected many Greek codices and set up a printing-press in the episcopal palace in order to have some of them edited. In this way works by Chrysostom, Basil, and Eusebius of Caesarea, as well as some devotional writings were published. It is interesting to note, and it adds to one's knowledge of Giberti's character, that there were also poets among the members of his household. Towards one of them, the erratic and puckish Francesco Berni, Giberti showed great forbearance and affection, but this extraordinary relationship did not last for more than a few years. A more permanent and less embarrassing guest was Marc-Antonio Flaminio. We have quoted above (Chapter 1) Flaminio's charming poem describing the kind of life that was lived in Bembo's orbit. Meanwhile Flaminio had written a good deal of religious poetry and had contributed to the general change of tone among the finest humanist spirits in Italy. (During the last stage of his life he was to pass from Giberti's household to that of Pole.)

One more strand of this complex and fruitful reform movement has still to be mentioned: the reform of the older monastic orders and the foundation of new ones. The revival of the Benedictines owed much to the activities of Abbot Gregorio Cortese, and there was a healthy stirring among Augustinians and Franciscans too. (The Franciscan reform led to the establishment of a new branch, the Capuchins.) Of the new orders founded during the first stage of the reform movement the most important was that of the Theatines. Its origin is intimately connected with the rise of an informal religious society called the Oratory of the Divine Love (c. 1517). Here, amidst all the distractions of Medicean Rome, an attempt was made by some fifty or sixty clerics to renew their inward lives by common prayer, meditation, and works of charity. Among the outstanding early members of the Oratory were Giberti, Caraffa, and the Italian nobleman Gaetano di Tiene. After a few years two of these men, Gaetano and Caraffa, went further than that. They obtained papal permission, not without some difficulties, to found the order of the Theatines (so called after the Latin name of Caraffa's episcopal see of Chieti). Gaetano and Caraffa gave up all their property and ecclesiastical benefices (these, in Caraffa's case, included an Archbishopric), and in September 1524 they and a few of their friends took the three solemn vows. The Theatines lived a common life and practised the most rigorous poverty, but they distinguished themselves from the older orders by wearing the ordinary clerical dress and by devoting themselves to ordinary clerical work: the administration of the sacraments, preaching, confessions, and all the other duties connected with the cure of souls. Soon they also took a leading part in ministering to the needs of the sick, particularly in the Hospitals for Incurables. The aim of this foundation was to produce a new *élite* of priests who could, by their example, contribute to a general religious awakening. The Theatines were so successful that their order became in effect a seminary, not indeed for parish priests, but for bishops.

Much of this success was due to the exceptional energy and devotion of the two founders, Gaetano and Caraffa. Rarely have collaborators been so dissimilar as these two. Of Gaetano it has been neatly said that he wished to reform the world, but without letting the world know that he was in it.[12] Caraffa, on the other hand, made it abundantly clear that he was in the world; in the course of his life the world had to take notice of him enough and to spare.[13] In him lived the fiery eloquence of the Neapolitan and the burning zeal of the religious fanatic. He was the oldest of all the reformers (he was seven years older than Contarini and twenty-four years older than Pole) and yet he outlived them all. Much more will have to be said about him at a later stage; as Pope Paul IV he was destined to have a most disturbing influence on Pole's life. Here it will suffice to draw attention to one feature that distinguished him from most men of this circle: unlike Contarini, Giberti, or Pole, Caraffa was not a humanist. True, he too knew the classical languages, and he had even at one time encouraged the work of Erasmus. But since then he had grown so single-minded that he had conceived a profound suspicion of humanist activities. To him, as to some contemporary Protestant fanatics, all this was vanity and a stumbling-block in the path of a Christian. During his papacy he caused all works of Erasmus, even those without any bearing on religion, to be put on the first Papal Index of forbidden books.

Meanwhile, however, Index and Roman Inquisition were still in the future; there was as yet no rift between the reformers. The unhappy papacy of Clement VII came to an end in September 1534, and in the following month Cardinal Alessandro Farnese became his successor as Paul III. His reign, which was to last for fifteen years, proved to be the long-awaited turning-point in the history of the Catholic Church. He began at once by making a strong declaration on Church reform. That, of course, had happened before, without any appreciable results, but we may imagine that the reformers everywhere began to take note when, in May 1535, a cardinal's hat was conferred on Gasparo Contarini. It was at about this time (1534–5) that Pole was gaining the friendship of the Venetian reformers by "continual and most familiar intercourse" with them.[14] Henceforth, Pole identified himself more and more with the work of these men. Their examples shaped the rest of his life.

The new Pope soon showed that his intentions were more serious than those of his predecessors, when he began, following Giberti's example, to reform his immediate surroundings. A universal reform was indeed impossible without a purge of the Curia and the ecclesiastical life of Rome, but that was particularly difficult because of the enormous number of ecclesiastical officials and hangers-on that had assembled in Rome. It is not surprising to learn that the moral and spiritual state of the Roman clergy was shockingly low. This appears from the terms of a papal edict dating from this period: Roman canons were reminded that they had to attend divine service; all priests were ordered to communicate on holidays of obligation and forbidden to visit taverns and brothels; and both clergy and laity were admonished to show due reverence in church and to abstain from soothsaying and the invocation of demons. Because so many priests had shown that they were incapable of saying Mass, provision was made for a special scrutiny of any priest before he was allowed to officiate in Rome. All this produced much opposition among the culprits; when some of the Cardinals were forbidden to take part in the Carnival they strongly resented this infringement of their liberty. In Rome, according to a telling jest, lived the worst men in the world, and worse than the others were the priests, and the worst of the priests were made Cardinals, and the worst of all the Cardinals was made Pope.[15]

This time, however, not the worst of the Cardinals had been made Pope. Paul III invited the newly created Cardinal Contarini to take up residence in the Vatican Palace, and for a time Contarini exercised a decisive influence on the course of the reform proceedings. It was he who suggested the immediate summoning of a special reform commission. Accordingly, in July 1536, invitations were sent out to the most prominent reformers—Caraffa, Cortese, Giberti, Sadoleto—and to their common friend, Reginald Pole. These men, together with Contarini and three other prelates, assembled in Rome early in November 1536, and within three months they produced a thoroughgoing and epoch-making document, the "Consilium de Emendanda Ecclesia."[16] It matters little who were the actual authors of this report; there can be no doubt that all the nine signatories contributed to it and shared the responsibility for its contents.

The preamble of the "Consilium" does not waste much time with generalities but states the two main principles of reform clearly and bluntly. The first one we have met already: rejection of the teaching that the Pope's will is law. "This is the Trojan horse," the reformers wrote, "out of which all the abuses and diseases have crept into the Church of God, and so it is through our guilt, ours we repeat, that the name of Christ is blasphemed among the unbelievers." The second principle was equally important: "The Vicar of Christ is not allowed to take any payment for the exercise of his power of the keys, entrusted to him by Christ. For this is Christ's injunction: Freely ye have received, freely give" (Matt. x, 8). Then follows a list of twenty-six abuses. Many of them refer to three particular evils: pluralism, non-residence, and various simoniacal practices. Here, for instance, is No. 8: "It is wrong that Cardinals should be bishops, sometimes controlling even more than one diocese. The offices of Cardinal and bishop are incompatible. A Cardinal must advise the Pope on the government of the whole Church, but a bishop must look after his flock, and this he cannot do unless he lives with his flock, like a shepherd with his sheep." And so from one abuse to another, in simple, straightforward language: priests were selected without care; monks lived scandalous lives; dispensations of almost any kind were freely sold; worship was neglected, etc. No one would wish to say that the content of the "Consilium" was original; that was not the intention of its authors. They merely summarized, fearlessly and comprehensively, what decent men had felt and said for a long time. "We have," the document concludes, "satisfied our consciences, with great hope that under your leadership, Holy Father, we shall see the Church of God purified and united, to the eternal glory of your name. You have taken the name of Paul. Paul was chosen as a vessel to carry the name of Christ to the Gentiles; you, we hope, have been chosen to revive in our hearts and deeds the forgotten name of Christ, to heal our sickness, to re-unite Christ's flock in one fold, and to avert from us the wrath of God, His well-merited vengeance, which is hanging over our heads, ready to fall."

II. *The Personal Conflict*

Here, at any rate, was a statement that was adequate to the sombreness of the religious situation. To be asked to co-operate in such an enterprise must have seemed to Pole the fulfilment of his boldest wish. But he could not accept this task with an untroubled mind. The year that preceded the summoning of the reform commission was one of uncommon anxiety to him; he was not allowed to forget the affairs of his native country and his conflict with Henry VIII. Pole's very absence from England seemed, and indeed was, a reflection on Henry's policy. So far Pole had kept silent about the far-reaching measures adopted by Henry since 1532: the annulment of his marriage with Katharine, the marriage with Anne Boleyn, and the open breach with the Pope. But such silence was intolerable to Henry; in this he foreshadowed the modern totalitarian state. It was, we remember, Thomas More's desire to remain silent that brought him to the block. Pole was not within Henry's direct reach, but the King was determined to make him speak, in one way or another. This fateful attempt to force the issue played a decisive part in Pole's life; we must now trace its successive stages and try to interpret Pole's complex reactions.

It was all bound up with the career of Thomas Starkey. We have noted above that Starkey left Pole towards the end of 1534 and became one of the King's chaplains. Starkey may have believed that he owed this advancement to his ability and to the learning he had acquired during his studies, but the truth was that Thomas Cromwell, to whom, as the present distributor of favours and promotions, he had turned in the first place, saw that Starkey's services could be used in the "affaire Pole." On 15 February 1535, Starkey, at the King's express command, wrote to Pole asking him for his opinion on the King's marriage and on the authority of the Pope, "for," he explained, "as much as you ever have used this prudent silence never to disclose your sentence and mind but in time and place I could not of your opinion anything therein plainly affirm."[17] Four years earlier, it is true, Pole had written a private letter to the King dissuading him from the divorce (see Chapter 2), but this letter had discussed merely the expediency of these proceedings, not their legality. A statement of principle was now demanded of Pole, on the divorce as well as on the whole

dispute with the Pope. In a further letter Starkey formulated
the two questions in the manner of school-problems: "Does
divine law allow the marriage of a widow whose first marriage
was consummated, with the brother of her first husband? Is
the superiority which the Roman bishop has claimed for many
centuries based on divine law?"[18]

Not content with putting these questions to Pole, Starkey
also suggested the right answers, supporting them with a
number of learned arguments. Now Starkey, as we have seen,
was no fool, and his arguments were well considered and
substantial. We need not repeat his views on Henry's matri-
monial problems; they followed the well-known pattern of the
royal apologists. But his views on the supremacy of the Pope
are interesting; they could not be lightly dismissed by Pole.
Granted, he argued, that the Papacy was a convenient institution for the preservation of spiritual unity, was it at all con-
ducive to political unity? Was it not rather a perpetual source
of discord among Christian princes? Had not Christ proclaimed
"My kingdom is not of this world"? Had it not therefore
been Christ's intention to leave everything *in* this world to the
"governance of man"? (In this context Starkey referred Pole
to the works of Marsilius of Padua, one of the true ancestors
of this trend of thought.) Starkey's view comes to something
like this: the Papacy in its present form, whatever its theoretical
nature may be, is primarily a secular power directed by an
Italian prince whose overweening ambitions must be curbed.
(The uncomfortable amount of truth contained in this statement was not likely to be missed by a friend of Contarini's.)
The ordering of all affairs, including the supervision of the
Church, belongs to the openly secular state, not to a power
which, under the cover of a spurious spiritual prestige, pursues
its all-too-secular ends and has thus helped to bring about the
break-up of Christendom. And this break-up has come to
stay; any hopes for the restoration of the old unity are expressly
rejected in one of Starkey's letters, even in the event of Contarini's elevation to the Papacy.[19]

Pole's first reaction to the royal request transmitted to him by Starkey was to play for time. He replied that he would answer Starkey's questions, but that they were of such weight as to require an extraordinary amount of study and thought.[20] As a matter of fact it took him well over a year from the receipt of Starkey's first letter before his answer was dispatched to England, in the form of a large book. Meanwhile he assuaged Henry's impatience by writing reassuring letters home. Starkey himself was convinced that Pole's eventual answer would be favourable to Henry, and so was Starkey's chief informant in Italy, who put down Pole's secretiveness in this matter to his wish that the King should be the first reader of his answer. And Pole himself asked Cromwell, on 28 October 1535, to assure the King of his "readiness to do him service at all times."[21]

Was Pole dissembling all the time and deliberately using ambiguous statements? Not, at any rate, in the beginning. It seems that Pole was simply not ready for a decisive action when Starkey's letter arrived. This reluctance to commit himself when faced with a sudden demand for action is borne out by other incidents in his life; it is, after all, a not altogether un-English trait of his character. He was bound to know that this decision would mould the rest of his life. Moreover, his deliberations were complicated by the fact that at this very time he was approached by a Spanish agent, who wished to draw him into the hazardous game of high politics.

This was a certain Martin de Çornoça, a political busybody, who suggested to his master, the Emperor Charles V, that Pole should be assigned an important part in a large-scale invasion of England; he assured the Emperor that England was on the brink of a revolution.[22] Charles V, in the midst of multifarious business concerning an empire on which the sun never set, did not attach much importance to these vague proposals of a minor official, but he did, at any rate, make inquiries about them with his ambassador in England, who, surprisingly, concurred with his colleague's views in every

GASPARO CONTARINI

by Alessandro Vittoria

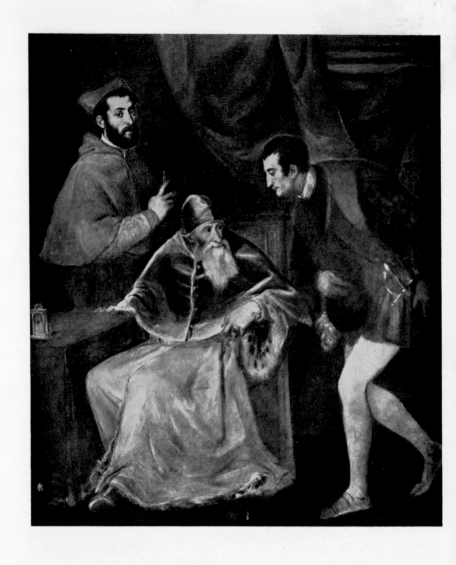

POPE PAUL III AND HIS NEPHEWS

from a painting by Titian

respect.[23] At this stage the Emperor seems to have asked
Çornoça to get in touch with Pole (all the earlier steps in this
matter had been undertaken without Pole's knowledge). Pole
honestly records his first reaction when he was approached in
the early months of 1535: it was one of sorrow that the pleasant
leisure hours ("mio dolce otio") which he was passing in
Venice would be suddenly interrupted. He was not prepared
to take part in any fantastic enterprises, but he agreed to send
a personal messenger to the Emperor, with a private plan of
his own. In his covering letter, dated 17 June 1535, he wrote:
"I humbly entreat Your Majesty to try peaceful means first . . .
before having recourse to arms."[24]

What were these peaceful means? We do not know since
Pole was too careful to commit them to paper. The only hint
we have is contained in a letter of Contarini's to the Emperor,
in support of Pole's scheme. "Pole," Contarini wrote, "thinks
of nothing save doing some act by which God and the whole
of Christendom may be benefited. Regardless of fatigue or of
danger to his person, and following the example of the early
Christians, he counts it great gain to suffer for Christ's sake."[25]
Did Pole intend to go to England at the risk of martyrdom
(More and Fisher were already in the Tower), in the hope of a
last-minute conversion of the King by a personal appeal with
the backing of the Emperor? This possibility gains some
support from the fact that about this time some members of
Pole's household seem to have envisaged his imminent return
to England.[26] Whatever the nature of Pole's plan, the Emperor
evidently did not think much of it. Wait and see, together with
non-committal thanks for Pole's suggestion, was the gist of his
answer, which took him over three months to dispatch;[27] no
more was heard of this project after this damping reply. Pole
probably did not know at the time that His Sacred Catholic
Majesty, so far from wishing to oppose the schismatical King
of England, was about to arrange a marriage between his own
brother-in-law Dom Luiz of Portugal and Henry's daughter
Mary, but the general rapprochement between the two mon-

F

archs did not escape his notice. This experience helped to produce his disillusioned conviction that the kings, bent on war and conquest, were not likely to render disinterested service to the cause of the Church.[28]

When Pole had to wait all through the summer for the Emperor's reply, he must have begun to realize the hopelessness of this approach. Meanwhile, he had to make up his mind how to deal with Henry's dangerous request. He spent most of the summer in Priuli's villa near Treviso, unable to think of anything else. Once again, he had to face the conflict between various considerations of expediency and a higher duty, dimly sensed at first but becoming clearer in the course of a prolonged inner struggle, which lasted "not for one night, as Jacob's wrestling with the Angel, but for many nights and days."[29] Self-love, as he calls it, and the love of his family counselled him to submit or to be silent. His duty—an utterly painful duty—he found to lie in a different direction.

During this time of anguish the news reached him of John Fisher's and Thomas More's execution. Had it now come to that? Henry had murdered two of the greatest and saintliest men of that age and indeed of all ages. We need not doubt Pole's word that writing about More's death brought to his eyes involuntary tears which made it difficult for him to go on with the composition of his treatise.[30] The martyrdom of these men, Pole believed, had manifested the truth of their cause, for this was God's method of declaring and confirming the secrets of His will, by the death first of His own Son and afterwards by the legions of martyrs; the deaths of Fisher and More were arguments written by the hand of God Himself in letters of blood.[31] The death of More, in particular, must have struck Pole with the force of a personal experience. More had embodied the ideal of his youth—an ideal which Pole had not always fully and clearly borne in mind. More's death revealed the complete significance of that unique life, which now became a "symbol perfected in death" and thus a guiding light to Pole in his own hour of darkness.

The King whom Pole had loved and whom he still loved (he had only just described him to Charles V as "endowed by God with all qualities and parts which constitute a great and religious prince")[32] had now committed an outrage which for the first time revealed the depth of his brutality. Due weight must be given to this revelation in discussing the reasons for Pole's final decision, but the root causes lie deeper still. He had been asked two questions; was he quite sure about the right answers to them? The problem of the divorce, we may assume, no longer caused him great trouble, but the Papacy was altogether a different matter. There is no reason to doubt Starkey's testimony that Pole had at first believed the supremacy of the Pope to be of human, not of divine, origin.[33] So, it should be remembered, had Thomas More.[34] Pole had had various opportunities, ever since his Paduan student days, of watching the Papacy at fairly close quarters, and much of what there was to see was bound to appal him. An unbiased observer of the Renaissance Papacy could be forgiven for not being able to believe in its divine origin. It is in this context that Pole's contact with the beginning of Church reform is of outstanding importance. He was thus enabled to see the Papacy, not as it still was in the year 1535, but as it would be in the future after the reform which had set in with Contarini's raising to the purple—an event which Pole ascribed to the direct intervention of God.[35] Now he could see the affairs of England in their true perspective (the same that More revealed to his judges that very summer). "Our evils—I am referring to the evils of England," he wrote to Priuli, "are not really ours; they are the evils of the whole Church."[36] And so, on 4 September, he began to write his answer to Henry's questions, intending "to render Peter's bark safe against any piratical attack."[37] In May 1536 he sent his letter, which had grown into a large book, to the King.

Pole had come to the conclusion that the only means of salvation lay in the reform of the traditional Church and in the restoration of the old spiritual unity among Christians. He had therefore spoken his mind about Henry's schism. For the rest, he was anxious to take his part in the great reform work which aimed at a spiritual rebirth of the Church; nothing short of this would do. Hard work lay ahead of him, much sorrow, much disappointment. But he had, at last, chosen. He was now thirty-five years old, "nel nezzo del cammin," and during much of his previous life he had been in a "dark wood." He had now emerged from it into the light of day.

NOTES TO CHAPTER FOUR

[1] F. Dittrich, *Regesten und Briefe des Kardinals Gasparo Contarini* (1881), p. 270. For Contarini in general, see F. Dittrich, *Kardinal Contarini* (1885)—by far the best account.

[2] Contarini, *Opera* (1571), p. 229.

[3] L. v. Ranke, *Die römischen Päpste* (7. Auflage, 1878), p. 82.

[4] On 4th January, 1529: Dittrich, *Regesten*, pp. 41–6.

[5] Le Plat, *Monumentorum ad historiam concilii Tridentini illustrandam spectantium amplissima collectio* (1781–7), vol. ii, pp. 608–15.

[6] Contarini, op. cit., pp. 402, 406, 407, 411.

[7] There is an excellent and comprehensive English account of Giberti by M. A. Tucker (*English Historical Review*, 1903, pp. 24 seq., 266 seq., 439 seq.). Cf. G. B. Pighi, *G. M. Giberti* (1924).

[8] Tucker, op. cit., p. 452.

[9] L. Pastor, *History of the Popes*, ed. R. F. Kerr (1923), vol. x, p. 428.

[10] For further details on Giberti's reforms, cf. Giberti, *Opera*, ed. Ballerini (1733), pp. 1–153.

[11] Francesco Zini, quoted in Pastor, op. cit., vol. x, p. 439.

[12] Ranke, op. cit., p. 92.

[13] As far as I know there is no adequate biography of Caraffa in any language. For some aspects of his life and work, cf. the various monographs by Dom R. Ancel.

[14] *S.P. Span.*, vol. v, part 1, No. 172.

[15] Pastor, op. cit., vol. xi, pp. 149, 152, 563, 568; Poggio, *Facetiae* (transl. Storer), p. 37.

[16] Reprinted in B. J. Kidd, *Documents illustrative of the Continental Reformation* (1911), pp. 307–18.

[17] *England in the Reign of King Henry VIII* (ed. Herrtage, Early English Text Society, 1873), part 1, p. xiv.

[18] Herrtage, op. cit., pp. xviii–xix.

[19] Herrtage, op. cit., pp. xix, xxii, xxv.

[20] *L. + P.*, vol. viii, Nos. 801, 1156.

[21] *L. + P.*, vol. ix, Nos. 1029, 701.

22 *S.P. Span.*, vol. v, part 1, No. 80.

23 *S.P. Span.*, vol. v, part 1, No. 109.

24 *S.P. Span.*, vol. v, part 2, No. 63. (This letter is wrongly dated in this Calendar.) Translation from Add. MSS., 28590, f. 6a (Brit. Mus.).

25 *S.P. Span.*, vol. v, part 1, No. 172 (dated 5 June, 1535, only twelve days before Pole's letter to the Emperor). Translation from Add. MSS., 28587, f. 323b (Brit. Mus.).

26 *L. + P.*, vol. viii, No. 581, vol. ix, No. 127.

27 *S.P. Span.*, vol. v, part 2, No. 109. (This letter, the answer to No. 63, is wrongly dated too.)

28 *Q.*, vol. i, p. 451.

29 *Q.*, vol. iv, p. 334.

30 Pole, *Pro Unitatis Ecclesiasticae Defensione* (1555), fol. 66b. Pole was, of course, well informed about More's trial and death. At that time he was also engaged on an Italian translation of an account of More's and Fisher's sufferings (*Opus Epistolarum Des. Erasmi Roterodami*, ed. P. S. Allen, vol. xi, p. 1259, note).

31 *Q.*, vol. i, p. 70.

32 On 17th June, 1535: *Cal. S.P. Span.*, vol. v, part 2, No. 63. Fisher was executed on 22nd June, More on 6th July.

33 Herrtage, op. cit., part 1, p. xxxviii.

34 R. W. Chambers, *Thomas More* (1935), p. 196. It so happens that this information comes from Pole himself who had it from More's friend Antonio Bonvisi: Strype, *Ecclesiastical Memorials* (1822), vol. iii, part 2, pp. 491–3.

35 *Q.*, vol. i, p. 450.

36 *Q.*, vol. i, p. 449.

37 *Q.*, vol. i, p. 427.

CHAPTER FIVE

THE BOOK AND THE CONSEQUENCES
(1536–1541)

IT would be idle to pretend that Pole's book, generally known under the name *De Unitate*, has been unjustly neglected by posterity. It is monstrously long, liberally sprinkled with irrelevant matter, and very repetitive. It is difficult to see why Pole who, on occasions, was not quite oblivious of literary requirements, did not cut it down to half its size or even less (the manuscript of what, after all, was supposed to be a "letter," runs to 280 folio pages). The tone, too, is of a kind that does not make for pleasant reading: it is invariably didactic and at times downright pedantic. But there are a number of very vigorous passages and some which are genuinely witty, and the part on Thomas More's life and martyrdom is outstanding in manner as well as in matter.

Pole's treatise can be divided into two parts. One of them deals more directly with Henry and his policy, while the other is meant to establish the primacy of the Pope and to demolish the idea of a secular headship of the Church. The arguments on the main problem inevitably follow the lines laid down in Thomas More's answer to his judges on 1 July 1535: "I am not bounden, my Lords, to conform my conscience to the council of one realm against the general council of Christendom. For I have, for every bishop of yours, above one hundred; and for one council of yours I have all the councils made these thousand years."[1] Some of these bishops and councils are expressly appealed to in Pole's book. It was really not a very hard task to show that Henry VIII was the first king ever to claim the headship of a Christian Church, and on the Papal supremacy, too, the weight of traditional opinion was overwhelming. Naturally, Pole makes constant use of the two most relevant Gospel passages: "Thou art Peter," and Christ's repeated injunction to His chief apostle: "Feed my sheep."

While Pole was writing this book, the work of one of Henry's apologists was sent to him, the *Oratio de dignitate et potestate regis*, by Richard Sampson, Bishop of Chichester. A large part of Pole's book is taken up by attacks on this work which, Pole punningly suggests, was not written by a Samson, but rather by a Goliath, the enemy of the sons of Israel. Bishop Sampson was altogether an easy target for Pole. A morally depraved Pope, runs one of Sampson's arguments, cannot possibly be the successor of St. Peter. Then what about a morally depraved bishop? is Pole's retort. And he goes on to ask, still more pertinently: what about a morally depraved King? Can he, of all people, be the Pope's successor as supreme head of the Church?[2]

Henry's moral depravity was evidently something that Pole had come to accept as a fact, and a deeply disturbing one at that. The King, Pole states at the very beginning of his treatise, is suffering from a grave illness, and much of what follows is expressly intended as a cure for this moral disease. In order to make the patient aware of his illness, the "doctor" uses the strongest language. This is how he addresses the King in a crucial passage towards the end: "You have squandered a huge treasure; you have made a laughing-stock of the nobility; you have never loved the people; you have pestered and robbed the clergy in every possible way; and lately you have destroyed the best men of your kingdom, not like a human being, but like a wild beast." This, Pole continues, is the sum total of Henry's actions during the twenty-seven years of his rule; nothing else, unless Henry repents, will have to be inscribed on his tombstone, except that one might add: "He has spent enormous sums to make all universities declare him incestuous."[3]

Pole's book contains much personal invective of this kind;

Henry is also called a robber, a murderer, and a greater enemy to Christianity than the Turk. Did Pole really hope that such language would have the required effect on Henry? Both Contarini and Priuli, to whom Pole had shown the various parts of his treatise as he was writing them, expressed their doubts about the bitterness of the tone. Pole may have made some minor corrections on their advice, but in the main he adhered to his text. He had little hope that the King could be converted by any treatise, whatever its tone; "nothing will have an effect on him," he added, "except a calamity, or something that makes him afraid."[4] We are, in fact, entitled to believe that Pole was not expecting any immediate results from his *magnum opus.* The sending of it to the King may have been bad psychology (though such a judgment would presuppose a clearer knowledge of Henry's character than we possess), but it is a misunderstanding to call it bad politics; it was not meant as a political move at all.

Pole's invectives called forth Starkey's comment: "[This is] the most frantic judgment that ever I read of any learned man in my life."[5] Starkey was shocked by Pole's bold language to his sovereign and posterity will not necessarily share this pious horror. Yet the word "frantic" does, in a sense, apply to this work; the unrestrained torrent of words betrays great restlessness in the writer. We know that Pole was far from being quiet in his mind while he was composing the book. To the causes for his mental anguish must be added the kind of self-reproach that is implied in his allusion to himself as one "who has so far been silent, who has always submitted to fear."[6] Had he perhaps been cowardly all this time? Had he not wasted many years in idle leisure, while men like More and Fisher, accepting the responsibilities of their stations, were setting out on their *via dolorosa?* True, he had occasionally whispered something in the ear of his sovereign, but now the time for whispering had passed: now only the loudest trumpets would do. Hence those jarring notes in Pole's treatise—a likely result when a naturally retiring and hesitant man forces himself, at long last, to make a decisive stand.[7]

Pole's difficulties must have been greatly enhanced by his complicated attitude to Henry VIII. We have several times alluded to this relationship, but we must now try to define its nature more precisely. That there was a certain mutual affection between them is beyond doubt, and Henry's initial liking for his younger cousin is not in any way problematic. But Reginald's relation to Henry was determined from the outset by the enchantment of distance. First at Oxford, then at Padua, Henry figured for him as the generous benefactor and embodiment of all princely virtues, and even in later and maturer years Pole did not see much of Henry at close quarters. In his treatise Pole uses a number of expressions which denote an earlier feeling of veneration and worship for Henry.[8] This, it might be suggested, was an obvious way of sugaring the all-too-bitter pill. It is therefore all the more remarkable that he used exactly the same words over twenty years later, many years after Henry's death, in an unpublished and undispatched letter to Caraffa. In this context, which did not necessitate any reference to Henry at all, Pole declared that Henry was one of the two men he had worshipped ("coluissem") more than any others (the second being Caraffa himself).[9] The recurrence of the word "worship" matters a great deal. If it had been a question of *love*, Contarini could not have been left out in this statement, but here a different feeling called for expression. And it was precisely this feeling that was so cruelly hurt by Henry's outrage against Fisher and More. A romanticized Henry now revealed himself in a wholly unexpected light—one that was not so surprising to a shrewder observer like More who knew that "if his head would win the King a castle in France it should not fail to go."[10] When Pole's earlier enchantment was followed by a sudden and irrevocable disenchantment, the resulting state of his mind was likely to be unbalanced in the extreme.

The breach with Henry was followed by further painful separations. Starkey severed all connections; Tunstall, the learned Bishop of Durham, expressed his strong disapproval. These former friends of Pole's were by no means Protestants, either now or later. They remained staunch Catholics in their other doctrines, but they accepted the ecclesiastical supremacy of the King. They refused to follow Pole in ascribing a decisive importance to the martyrdoms of Fisher and More or indeed in regarding their deaths as martyrdoms at all. For the first time Pole was faced with that confusion of tongues that was to dominate his century more and more. "We are brought to such case," he complained in his reply to Tunstall, "worse than Babylon, that no man understands another in his own tongue. What one calls captivity, another calls liberty; [what] one says is against the King, another calls with the King."[11]

Still, in his contest with his former friends he had no doubt about the rightness of his own position and there was no need to feel responsible for them. The case of his family was different. He received letters from his mother and his elder brother, imploring him to change his mind and not to accept the Pope's invitation to come to Rome. These letters were bound to move him very much, threatening as they did the severance of all natural bonds. When Pole received them he had already set out on his journey to Rome. He now seriously considered turning back and would probably have done so, had it not been for his travelling companions, Giberti and Caraffa, who helped him to overcome his vacillations.[12] And so the three of them continued their journey to Rome, the restless Caraffa urging them on like Mars, Giberti proceeding more slowly like Saturn, and "Signor Rainaldo, like Mercury, accommodating himself now to the one, now to the other."[13]

Towards the end of October 1536 they arrived in Rome. Pole was given rooms in the Vatican, right above the Pope's own apartment, and began to wear ecclesiastical dress.[14] His taking of holy orders could now be only a question of time. From early November onwards rumours were circulating about important additions to the College of Cardinals, and Pole's name was mentioned in this connection. Pole, however, showed his usual reluctance to accept a public office. He pointed out to the Pope that his being raised to the purple, at that time, would make him appear too closely bound to the Pope's interests and would endanger his relatives. At first the Pope accepted these arguments and promised to defer the promotion. But on the very day of the nomination (22 December 1536) he suddenly changed his mind. He sent his private Chamberlain to Pole's room, to acquaint him of this decision. To avoid any further resistance he took the precaution to send a barber along at the same time, who was to put Pole's tonsure in order. The victim, according to his first biographer who was present, was clearly perturbed and displeased, but eventually submitted "like a lamb to the shearer."[15] Together with Pole, eleven others were created Cardinals on that day, among them Sadoleto and Caraffa.

It is now impossible to unravel the motives that caused the Pope's sudden change of mind, but it is practically certain that political considerations were among them. That very winter (at various dates in October) large parts of the North of England rose against Henry VIII. Religious and social elements were inextricably combined in this revolt which is usually called the "Pilgrimage of Grace." Many of the rebels' demands showed their anxiety for the maintenance of the ancient faith; in particular, they protested against the dissolution of the monasteries. There can be no doubt that this rising constituted a serious threat to Henry's power. The Pope considered this an opportune moment to nominate a Legate for England, who was to exploit this situation and force Henry back into the Church. The Pope's choice was an obvious one: the newly created Cardinal Pole. On 18 February 1537 Pole left Rome to take up his legatine duties, accompanied by Giberti, the experienced Papal diplomat.

Here a word is necessary about the moral implications of Pole's mission. From this time onwards Pole is usually referred to in contemporary English documents as a "traitor," and this charge, in one form or another, has been repeated time and time again ever since. Did Pole's acceptance of this particular task amount to treason? No simple answer either way is possible. From the point of view of the nascent modern state he was a traitor, from the point of view of traditional Christendom he was not. Henry himself stated the issue symbolically when, 1538, he desecrated the memory of Thomas à Becket and declared him "a rebel who fled the realm to France and to the Bishop of Rome to procure the abrogation of wholesome laws."[16] Whatever the real issue between Becket and his King may have been, Henry VIII evidently saw it in the light of his own struggle with the Papacy and with another rebel who had fled to the Bishop of Rome. Pole's case stands or falls with Becket's. The argument that Pole's Papacy was not the same as Becket's does not apply because Pole's vision penetrated beyond the Papacy of his day to its spiritual restoration.

Perhaps we are in a better position to appreciate the true complexity of the problem than our fathers and grandfathers whose thought was hardly able to transcend the modern state. In an earlier chapter of this study a good deal of space has been devoted to a discussion of Pole's political views. One of his fundamental convictions, we found, was the limitation of the monarch's will by law (positive, natural, or divine) and the resulting right of resistance against a lawless ruler. He made it abundantly clear in his book that he considered Henry as a law-breaker of the first order and that the English people had the right to rebel against the tyrant. In the Pilgrimage of Grace some of them had, indeed, drawn this conclusion for themselves. In their own eyes, and in Pole's, they were not traitors but restorers of law. Therefore Pole demanded in his book that the traditional Head of the Christian Church should excommunicate Henry, the ecclesiastical usurper. It was common knowledge that a bull of excommunication had been ready for some time. According to the terms of this bull the King of England, unless he repented within three months, was declared deposed; his subjects were absolved from their oath of obedience; and foreign nations were forbidden intercourse with the supporters of the schism.[17] The publication of the bull was postponed for political reasons, but its terms were certainly not considered fantastic by Pole's contemporaries. Henry, of course, and his supporters denied the Pope's right to censure a reigning monarch, but this was then, and remained for some time, a minority view. All this needs stating with precision and emphasis, because any similar connection with the Papacy has been regarded as treasonable in this country for such a long time that a determined effort is necessary to arrive at a dispassionate view. To Pole, loyalty to the King and country was not an empty word; it was not, however, the highest loyalty he knew. Like Thomas More, he regarded himself as the "King's good servant, but God's first."

We know that this conflict caused Pole much distress, and that it was bound up with the fundamental conflict of his early life: "vita activa" against a *soi-disant* "vita contemplativa." He had eventually chosen an active life in the service of a true contemplative ideal, but now he was to discover the particular difficulties of this choice—the fly in this particular ointment. He was to find that, in his special circumstances, the attempt to be "God's servant" would involve him, for a time at least, in international politics.

The political quarrels of an age, so absorbing to some contemporaries, are apt to leave posterity quite cold. And rightly so. The wearisome ups and downs of fortune, the negligible results of often superhuman efforts, tend to produce the impression of utter futility. We are often tempted to echo Dryden's address to his century:

> Thy wars brought nothing about,
> Thy lovers were all untrue.
> 'Tis well an old age is out
> And time to begin a new.

And then we always find that all the hopes of a new beginning turn to dust, as each new age becomes entangled in the same old futilities.

The political quarrels of Pole's age centred round the struggle of two dynasties, the Habsburgs and the Valois, represented by Charles V, the Holy Roman Emperor who was also ruler of the vast Spanish possessions, and Francis I, King of France. Ever since Charles' accession to the Imperial throne in 1519 there had been enmity between these monarchs whose interests clashed in many parts of Europe. They first fought for nine years, and after a respite war broke out again in 1536, a few months before Pole was sent on his mission. From this point of view the time was ill-chosen. Francis and Charles were engaged in a deadly struggle, and neither of them wished to make more enemies than was absolutely necessary. In the fog of diplomatic dealings and double-dealings one thing is perfectly clear: Francis and Charles could not afford to alienate Henry. Charles was actually negotiating with Henry a marriage between Princess Mary and his own brother-in-law, while Francis kept Henry informed of Pole's movements and plans. At the same time, the two Catholic monarchs wanted to remain on good terms with the Pope. Protesting their loyalty to the Vicar of Christ, they did not openly oppose his policy, but they refused to transact any official business with his legate, let alone publish his censures on Henry. The Pope was further handicapped by the bad reputation of Papal politics, owing to the equivocal conduct of so many of his predecessors. Francis, for example, expressed his suspicion that the whole matter of the Papal mission was nothing but an Imperialist manœuvre, and had to be reassured by the Papal nuncio "that the ways of his Holiness are not like those of Pope Clement."[18] The Papacy was now paying the price for centuries of secular power-politics and spiritual degradation.

The policy of Pope Paul III in this particular matter is not at all clear. Some observers believed that he intended to give direct support to the English insurgents, but in that case he need not have waited until February before he dispatched Pole on his mission. Moreover, he would have had to provide Pole with a great deal of money. That he omitted to do, and this omission was duly noted by the Emperor who consequently refused to attach much importance to the whole affair.[19] Pole had foreseen this point and asked the Pope for ample sums for his mission, without avail. It seems that the Pope's real intention did not amount to more than a diplomatic demonstration to frighten Henry and give moral support to the Northern rebels.[20]

Even so, it was a big blunder to delay Pole's departure until 18 February. By the end of that month Henry had managed, by fair means and foul, to suppress the Northern revolt. In this position he was not likely to be frightened by the Papal mission, particularly in view of the ignominious treatment of the legate by the two Continental rulers. Francis refused to see Pole and had him politely escorted out of his country, and Charles's deputy in Flanders did not allow him to come to Brussels, so that Pole had to take refuge in the technically neutral territory of the Cardinal Bishop of Liége. There he stayed for three months (May to August 1537) waiting in vain for a more hopeful turn of events.

Henry had won a resounding diplomatic victory. But he was not yet satisfied: he wanted to get hold of the legate himself—to have him, as he put it bluntly, "by some mean trussed up and conveyed to Calais"[21] and thence to England. He was no doubt motivated by a desire for revenge, but even more important than that may have been his wish to prevent the publication of Pole's book. There is ample evidence in the documents of the time that Henry greatly feared such a publication; it is indeed remarkable, and proof of Pole's freedom from malice, that he never took this step at all.[22] Henry surrounded Pole with spies; he hired kidnappers and cut-throats; and it is said that he offered the Emperor a large auxiliary force in exchange for Pole's person.[23] All these attempts came to nothing, but the necessary precautions added to the indignity of Pole's situation. He was thus forced to return to Rome, travelling by a devious and unusual route.

For fundamentally the same reasons a second mission undertaken about a year later was destined to fail. In June 1538 the old adversaries Francis and Charles concluded a ten years' truce at Nice. A few months later the Pope decided to issue the long-delayed bull of excommunication against Henry, and in view of the recent pact he ventured to hope that Francis and Charles would publish the bull in their realms and break off all commercial relations with the schismatic King of England. More than that, the Pope explained, was not expected of them; a military intervention was not in any way envisaged. Once again Pole was sent on a legatine mission, and once again he came up against the same wall. To us who have had some experience of non-aggression pacts and economic sanctions, this need not be a cause for surprise. The Emperor, whom Pole visited in Toledo, poured scorn on the Pope's proposals. Pole confessed that he could not fathom the Emperor's mind, and for that he may be forgiven; it is unlikely that the Emperor himself could always carry in his head the whole maze of schemes and policies that constituted his life. The plain truth is that the pact of Nice was not built on solid foundations and that the Emperor was therefore reluctant to break with Henry; within only three years the war with France broke out afresh. Francis, for his part, did not even receive the legate. He sent word that he was prepared to do exactly as much as the Emperor—in the circumstances a rather discouraging message. Pole spent six months in Carpentras with his old friend Sadoleto, and then, carefully avoiding Henry's assassins, he returned to Rome towards the end of 1539, defeated and humiliated for the second time within a few years.

It will appear from this brief account of Pole's legations that it would be absurd to blame him for their failure. Even if he had been gifted with Talleyrand's diplomatic ability, the outcome could not have been different. Some historians have used these proceedings as evidence for Pole's inability to grasp worldly matters. Such a judgment implies a serious misunderstanding. Pole was quite capable of grasping political issues, but he was not willing to take part in the futile political game. True, he had hoped that the Emperor, faithful to his ancient office, would defend the Church against a schismatic king; this hope was shared by others, including such experienced men as Contarini, Giberti, and the Pope himself. But now Pole became more firmly convinced than ever that, of all causes, the cause of religion was the worst-served of all; and this, he added ironically, in spite of the daily prayers to God "Thy will be done."[24] It was this conviction that enabled him, some years later, to warn the Council of Trent against "spiritual wickedness in high places" and to draw a sharp distinction between the service of God and the service of princes.[25] These views of an honest and sensitive observer are worth pondering. The so-called "Realpolitiker" should not be given the credit, as his name implies, for being a realist; judgments such as Pole's show a wider and profounder grasp of reality than the short-sighted and short-lived calculations that usually pass for political wisdom.

While it must be stressed that Pole was not a political simpleton, it seems hardly necessary to refute the opposite view that he was an incessant political plotter—a view that has been put forward by such serious historians as Froude and Hook. His whole life is surely a sufficient refutation of it. Only on one more occasion did he accept a legatine mission, and that was not primarily a political task. Nor was he a kind of "Grey Eminence," intriguing behind the scenes; he was by no means popular among the politicians of the age. He was in fact happiest whenever he could withdraw from the political scene, and he did so as soon as the slightest opportunity offered. During his stay at Liége in 1537, and again two years later in Carpentras, he led a semi-monastic life of study and devotion, surrounded by a circle of like-minded friends. In Carpentras he discussed religious matters with Sadoleto and read the psalms with Priuli and others. His life in Liége is vividly described in one of Priuli's letters. "In the morning," Priuli writes, "everyone remains in his room until an hour and a half before dinner, when we assemble in the private chapel for the recitation of the office according to the rules of the Theatines. Bishop Giberti is our master of ceremonies [Maestro di capella]. After the office we hear Mass, and then we dine. During dinner-time there is a reading from St. Bernard, and conversation. After dinner the Bishop usually reads a chapter from Eusebius. . . . In the evening we sing Vespers and Compline, and then, every other day, the legate [Pole] lectures to us on the epistles of St. Paul, beginning with the first epistle to Timothy. . . . How often has the legate said to me: 'Surely this peace is given to us by God!' And he always adds: 'Oh, why is not Mons. Contarini with us?'"[26]

Such spiritual refreshment must have been particularly welcome to Pole during those years, which brought him immeasureable sorrow and affliction. When Cromwell read Pole's book he threatened, with characteristic cruelty, that he would make the author "eat his own heart," and soon afterwards he indicated how he intended to do that: "Pity it is," he wrote to one of Pole's servants, "that the folly of one brainsick Poole, or to say better, of one witless fool, should be the ruin of so great a family."[27] Pole's family was to be the target for Cromwell's and Henry's merciless revenge. Many of Pole's relatives were in any case, like Pole himself, potential rivals of the Tudors; in one way or another they represented, or were suspected of representing, Yorkist claims to the throne. A long time before the King had declared that he meant to exterminate the "White Rose";[28] now he was going to fulfil this pledge.

The first step was the arrest, on 29 August 1538, of Sir Geoffrey Pole, the Cardinal's younger brother. Sir Geoffrey's nerves gave way under examination and he made a number of statements which incriminated Henry Pole, Lord Montague, the eldest of the three brothers, and Henry Courtenay, Marquis of Exeter, their cousin. On 4 November Montague and Exeter were committed to the Tower, and a month later they were charged with treason before the Lord High Steward and a jury of peers. The charge was based on a few stray remarks such as "I like well the proceedings of Cardinal Pole" and "Knaves rule about the King, I trust to give them a buffet one day." No treasonable actions had been discovered, no plots, no conspiracies. The verdict was prearranged. Exeter and Montague were condemned to death and beheaded on Tower Hill. With them a number of minor victims were put to death. Sir Geoffrey Pole was also condemned to death but pardoned because he had turned King's evidence against his kinsmen. Even Montague's son, still a child, was imprisoned in the Tower; he was never seen again. The extermination of the White Rose was proceeding with thoroughness.

These well-planned judicial murders, terrible counter-strokes against the "traitorous" Cardinal, were intended to rid the King of dangerous rivals who were also powerful magnates of the West Country. There was no stronger influence in Devon and Cornwall than that of the Courtenays, and the Poles counted for much in Dorset, Wiltshire, and Hampshire. Their retainers' gossip was apt to be unguarded—"the Marquis will wear the garland some day" and similar statements were picked up by informers and carefully noted in London.[29] Ten years later, during the formidable Western rising of 1549, the Poles were not yet forgotten in that part of the country; one of the rebels' demands ran as follows: "We think it very meet because the Lord Cardinal Pole is of the King's blood, [he] should not only have his free pardon, but also sent for to Rome and promoted to be first or second of the King's Council."[30]

After the executions were over, the events were carefully explained to the public, including, of course, the foreign ambassadors. One of them dryly remarked that this amounted to putting the accused on trial after their death.[31] Some treasonable correspondence was conveniently discovered (but not exhibited); Montague and Exeter were said to have conspired to kill the King and all his children, and to usurp the kingdom. All these lies were embodied in a semi-official publication, described by the King as a "pretty book" and entitled: *An Invective against the great and detestable vice, treason.* The author was Richard Morison—formerly a poor scholar whom

Reginald Pole had rescued from hunger and cold, but now in government service and on the way to influence and wealth. Morison had a ready wit and a facile pen, and was quite ready to use both of them on behalf of those who were prepared to pay the piper. From incidental statements in his pamphlet it appears that he may have been present at the trial. In any case, he was bound to know the gist of the facts; he cannot possibly have believed his own propaganda. When Pole's attention was drawn to Morison's book he made the character-istic remark: "I have read his writings more with pity than with indignation, because they show nothing but the miserable servitude of his mind." Morison was not the first, and not indeed the last, man of letters to show such servitude of mind. It was he, not the murdered men, who was really guilty of treason—of the all-too-frequent "trahison des clercs."

Morison, it might be said, was merely a paid scribbler and is now rightly forgotten. But the evil went deeper than that. It is really saddening to have to note, in this context, the temporary lapse of even so great a "clerk" as Hugh Latimer, the preacher and future martyr. He knew of Cromwell's intention to make Pole eat his own heart, and a few days after the execution of Pole's kinsmen he sent his congratulations to Cromwell ("the instrument of God" as he called him), cal-lously adding: "Pole must now eat his own heart and be [as] heartless as he is graceless."[32]

Pole had now lost his brother and his cousin, but worse was to follow. Henry did not spare the Countess of Salisbury, Pole's mother, then in her sixty-seventh year. In her case the political reasons that contributed to the death of her eldest son could not have played an important part, especially in view of her age; here, the desire for revenge predominated. In November 1538 the Countess was submitted to a searching examination. Absolutely nothing was found against her. In spite of this she was carried off, first to a private place of imprisonment and later to the Tower where she suffered much hardship from the cold owing to insufficient clothing. During her examination the old lady showed much steadfastness and dignity. When she was asked who had told her that the Cardinal had escaped assassination she admitted that her other sons had informed her about it, "and for motherly pity," she added, "I could not but rejoice." And to the question whether she had talked of Reginald being Pope one day and returning to England, she made the disarming reply: "I have often wished to see him again in England with the King's favour, though he were but a poor parish priest."[33] Her examiners gave her the grudging testimonial that she was "rather a strong and constant man than a woman."[34] Her last words to her eldest son must have been a great support to him in his hour of trial: "Son Montague, my advice in the case you stand in is to endeavour to serve your prince without disobeying God's commandment."[35] We may gather from this what, in her inmost heart, she thought of Reginald's decision to be the "King's good servant, but God's first."

Henry was determined to pursue his prey to the end. His next Parliament (April–May 1539) was made to pass a comprehensive Act of Attainder against the dead and the living alike. The executed men were included as well as Cardinal Pole and a number of others, among them Lady Salisbury. The only "evidence" against the Countess that Cromwell was able to produce was of the flimsiest kind: in one of her coffers a coat of arms had been found, showing on one side the English lion flanked by marigolds and pansies, and on the other side the wounds of Christ. The flowers were interpreted as standing for Cardinal Pole and Princess Mary, and the Five Wounds had figured on banners during the Pilgrimage of Grace. The implication was supposed to be clear beyond doubt: the Countess had participated in a plot to marry the Princess to the Cardinal and to raise them to the throne of England.[36] This fantastic charge sufficed to ensure the Countess' death sentence, which was not, however, carried out for fully two years. On 27 May 1541 the King had her beheaded in the Tower.

All the Cardinal's friends agreed in admiring his fortitude

of mind in the face of these terrible blows. His first biographer
was present when Pole heard of his mother's death. Pole
said: "Until now I thought that God had given me the grace
of being the son of one of the best and most honoured ladies in
England, . . . but now He has wished to honour me still more,
by making me the son of a martyr." Then he withdrew into
his private oratory, where he remained for about an hour,
coming out afterwards with his wonted serenity.[37] Pole did
not parade his grief in front of his friends, but we can gather
his feelings from a moving statement he made a few years
later, writing to Edward VI, after Henry's death. "When
your father," he told the young King, "ploughed me up with
the heavy ploughshare of his persecution, I found that I became
more capable of receiving the heavenly seed of faith, hope and
charity. Thus I became more apt for the study of divinity, not
indeed in human schools, from human teachers, but in the
school of God, from God Himself. . . . With the growth of
faith, hope and charity I began to enter into the mysteries of
the Holy Scriptures and the true meaning of other writings.
Hence I can truly say that the wrath of the King has profited
me more than his friendship. When I was studying the
humanities he gave me abundant help; yet he helped me even
more in my study of divinity, when he deprived me of all that
was dear to me and even tried to deprive me of my life."[38]

Reginald Pole had travelled far since his student days at the
University of Padua. The lessons he had learnt in the university
of life had been harder, but the truth that was now imprinted
on his mind was of a higher and more satisfying nature. Now,
also, he was more capable than before of handing on the truth,
of being a guide to others; it was this activity that brought him
consolation and a sense of fulfilment. And once again he was
privileged to enter into a spiritual relationship of great beauty.
A few years before, the fatherless exile had found a new father
in Gasparo Contarini; now, after the tragic loss of his mother,
he was to find a new mother in one of the "best and most
honoured ladies" in Italy, Vittoria Colonna.

NOTES TO CHAPTER FIVE

[1] R. W. Chambers, *Thomas More* (1935), p. 341.

[2] *Pro Unitatis Ecclesiasticae Defensione* (henceforth quoted as *De Unitate*) (Strasbourg, 1555), fols. 24a, 71a.

[3] *De Unitate*, fol. 83a.

[4] *Q.*, vol. i, pp. 436, 438.

[5] Strype, *Ecclesiastical Memorials* (1816), vol. vi, p. 31.

[6] *De Unitate*, fol. 76a.

[7] This psychological explanation was shrewdly hinted at by Starkey: Strype, op. cit., p. 39.

[8] *De Unitate*, fols. 2a, 2b. Cf. "Apologia ad Carolum Caesarem" (*Q.*, vol. i, p. 67): "amore ac veneratione"; "coluerit."

[9] Petyt MSS. 538, vol. 46, fol. 405a (Inner Temple Library, London).

[10] Roper's *Life of More* (Everyman's Library), p. 15.

[11] Strype, op. cit., p. 72 (wording slightly altered).

[12] *Q.*, vol. i, pp. 483–4.

[13] This vivid description comes from Abbot Gregorio Cortese, in his letter to Contarini, dated 8th October 1536: F. Dittrich, *Regesten und Briefe des Kardinals Gasparo Contarini* (1881), p. 92.

[14] *L. + P.*, vol. xi, No. 1160.

[15] *Q.*, vol. v, p. 365. It is easy to misunderstand the intervention of the barber. The tonsure cannot, of course, be *given* by a barber, only restored. This implies that Pole was no longer a layman, though he had not yet received any orders. He had probably received the tonsure, which made him into a "clericus," when he was at the University, as he was destined for the Church. Not even at that time could a layman, in this technical sense, have held the Deanery of Exeter and other ecclesiastical benefices. (I owe this interpretation to Fr. Philip Hughes.) On Caraffa's promotion, cf. Chapter 8, towards the end.

[16] *L. + P.*, vol. xiii, part 2, No. 848.

[17] Pastor, *History of the Popes*, vol. xii, p. 461.

[18] *L. + P.*, vol. xii, part 1, No. 675.

[19] *L. + P.*, vol. xii, part 1, No. 696.

[20] This, it seems, was Giberti's view: *L. + P.*, vol. xii, part 1, No. 1053. For Pole's first legation, cf. G. M. Monti, *Studi sulla Riforma Cattolica e sul Papato* (1941).

[21] 26th April, 1537: *L. + P.*, vol. xii, part 1, No. 1032.

[22] The book was set up in type in 1538 or 1539, without Pole's consent (*Q.*, vol. iv, pp. 340–1). In this form it was never published, but Pole seems to have given individual copies to some of his friends (cf. Dixon, *History of the Church of England*, vol. iv, p. 258); some of these (undated) copies survive. The Protestant Vergerio published the text in 1555 in Strasbourg, together with a bitter preface and some Lutheran writings; Catholic editions followed in 1569, 1587, and 1698. Gairdner (in *D.N.B.*) says that Pole published the book in 1554, but the letter referred to by him (*S.P. Ven.*, vol. v, No. 901) does not warrant such a conclusion.

[23] Beccadelli's Life (*Q.*, vol. v, p. 366) mentions 10,000 men for ten months (the Latin translation has 4,000 men: vol. i, p. 16). There seems to be no other record of this—not, perhaps, surprisingly.

[24] Letter to Contarini, 25th March, 1539: *Q.*, vol. ii, p. 149.

[25] Address to the Second Session of the Council of Trent, 7 January, 1546 (cf. Chapter 7 below).

[26] *Q.*, vol. ii, pp. civ–cv. This is confirmed by a recently discovered letter of Gerard Morinck: cf. H. de Vocht, *Monumenta Humanistica Lovaniensia* (1934), pp. 577–8.

[27] *L. + P.*, vol. xiii, part 2, No. 1036; vol. xii, part 2, No. 795. The spelling "Poole" is quite common; Cromwell's "rhyme" suggests the contemporary pronunciation of Pole's name.

[28] *L. + P.*, vol. xiii, part 2, No. 753.

[29] F. Rose-Troup, *The Western Rebellion of 1549* (1913), p. 25. The annual value of the Marquis of Exeter's lands amounted to £2,451 8s. 11¾d. (*Devon and Cornwall Notes and Queries*, vol. xviii, p. 211).

[30] Rose-Troup, op. cit., p. 223.

[31] *L. + P.*, vol. xiv, part 1, p. 72.

[32] *L. + P.*, vol. xiii, part 2, No. 1036.

[33] *L. + P.*, vol. xiii, part 2, No. 818.

[34] *L. + P.*, vol. xiii, part 2, No. 855.

[35] *L. + P.*, vol. xiii, part 2, No. 855.

[36] *L. + P.*, vol. xiv, part 1, No. 980.

[37] *Q.*, vol. v, p. 388.

[38] *Q.*, vol. iv, pp. 339–40.

CHAPTER SIX

FAITH, WORKS, AND JUSTIFICATION
(1541–1545)

IN August 1541 the Pope rewarded Pole's services by conferring on him the governorship of the "Patrimonium Petri," the oldest of the Papal states. This involved Pole's residence in Viterbo, forty miles north-west of Rome, and within an easy day's journey from the Curia, as the Pope courteously added, so that Pole was available for consultation whenever the need arose. This governorship was a post altogether after Pole's heart. The public duties were certainly not onerous (they did not take up more than one or two hours a day), nor were there any specially complicated problems to be solved. His main duty was the dispensing of justice, and that he liked. For the rest, his unspotted way of life was bound to set a good example and the gentleness of his temper was likely to make him popular. His tenure of office was uneventful— perhaps the best result any rule can hope to achieve. Some of Pole's detractors in the College of Cardinals even noted with disapproval that only very few people were put to death during his governorship. So far from regarding that as a fault, Pole suggested that gratitude was due to God for not having provided many occasions which called for severe punishments. It was ominous that Pole had to defend his leniency, despite the fact that no palpable evils had been caused by it.[1]

Pole's negligence was considered all the more serious because his household in Viterbo included two men who were suspected of heresy: Pietro Carnesecchi, who many years later was in fact executed for heresy, and Marc-Antonio Flaminio, the poet. Both of them had come for a time under the influence of Juan de Valdès, the teacher of the most prominent Italian Protestants. Flaminio did not show any inclination to separate from the Catholic Church, but he might have been driven to extremes had he been subjected to persecution. As it was, Pole's example and influence gave him the peace of mind that some of his friends could not find in the Catholic Church.[2] Pole, in his turn, valued Flaminio's spiritual gifts very highly. In December 1541 he wrote to Contarini that he spent much time "in the holy and useful company" of Carnesecchi and Flaminio. "I call it useful," he went on, "because of an evening Flaminio gives me and the greater part of my household a meal of that food which does not perish, in such a manner that I do not remember ever having felt greater consolation and edification."[3]

In addition to Carnesecchi and Flaminio, Pole's household consisted, as usual, of a miscellaneous collection of men, some of whom had lived with Pole for a considerable time. We meet again Bernardino, the old factotum, the English scholar George Lily, and of course the faithful Priuli. In addition we might note Thomas Goldwell, the first English Theatine and afterwards Bishop of St. Asaph, and Bartholomeo Stella, one of the earliest members of the Oratory of Divine Love. There must have been altogether about thirty members of Pole's "familia."[4] Of these, Priuli and Flaminio were his most intimate friends, but the closest and most significant relationship of all bound him to the celebrated poetess Vittoria Colonna, who arrived in Viterbo a few days after Pole and took up residence in the convent of St. Catherine.

Vittoria, ten years older than Pole, was now a woman of over fifty. Her early life had been outwardly splendid but not favoured with happiness. At nineteen she married Ferrante d'Avalos, better known as the Marchese di Pescara, but her husband, a brilliant soldier of rising fame, was not faithful to her and left her much alone. In 1525 Pescara died of the wounds he had received in the battle of Pavia; at thirty-five Vittoria was a widow. Meanwhile she had discovered her poetical talent and had entered into a number of literary friendships. For a time she devoted herself to celebrating her dead husband in poem after poem in the manner of Pietro Bembo, who was among her friends. These poems share the shortcomings of Bembo's own: they are all too smooth and almost devoid of true feeling. Her hero Pescara remains lifeless and indistinct; her endlessly reiterated worship of him does not carry conviction. But these poems were handed round in the literary circles of Italy and were given an unlimited welcome.

In some ways Vittoria's further progress was similar to Pole's. She, too, had to find her way through the glittering world of the Italian Renaissance, a world of confidently secular values; she, too, was for a time under Bembo's spell. Vittoria was also on friendly terms with Castiglione, whose *Cortegiano* she greeted with exaggerated praise. Soon, however, she came to penetrate beyond the boundaries of the *Cortegiano* into a territory that remained unknown to Castiglione and Bembo. Like Pole, she discovered new spiritual resources and began to take what part she could in Church reform, mainly by giving her support to the newly founded offshoot of the Franciscans, the Capuchins. From now on she often chose to live in convents, sharing the life of the nuns, and her poetry, like Flaminio's, became exclusively devoted to religious subjects. Not all of her later poems are free from the faults of the earlier ones, but some are of remarkable force. The best are both intensely felt and convincing.

In the 1530's Vittoria was often in Rome, and from 1538 to 1540 she lived there altogether. It was then that she acquired the friendship of the man whose name has carried hers across the ages: Michelangelo Buonarotti. We happen to possess reports of conversations between Vittoria and Michelangelo, held in a monastic garden overlooking Rome and in the nearby church. These conversations give us a lifelike picture of Vittoria's Roman circle, of her tact and graciousness, and of Michelangelo's depth. On one occasion, for example, the topic under discussion was religious art. Michelangelo insisted

that it was not the subject of a picture that mattered; it was
the laboriously achieved perfection of a work of art that could
awaken and refine true piety, for perfection was itself divine.
"A good picture," he added, "is nothing but a copy of God's
perfection, an imitation of His painting."[5]

These conversations were shared by a group of friends and
fellow-artists; for the more personal contact between Vittoria
and Michelangelo we must turn to their letters and poems.
How much Michelangelo owed to Vittoria can perhaps best be
gathered from one of his most moving sonnets.[6] In this poem,
which is addressed to Vittoria, he compares himself to the first
model that the sculptor shapes in worthless material, before
entrusting his idea to the more valuable stone. Then he
goes on:

> *Simil di me model nacqu'io da prima,*
> *Di me model per opra più perfetta*
> *Da voi rinascer poi, donna alta e degna.*

> First I was born a model of my self
> That later, as a perfect work of art
> You, gracious lady, might create me new.

"Create me new": these are weighty words, coming from
Michelangelo. There is bound to remain an element of
mystery in the relationship of these proudly reticent human
beings, but there can be no doubt that Michelangelo, at a
particularly difficult stage of his tormented life, derived new
strength from his friendship with the gentle Marchesa.

And Vittoria, also, was greatly enriched. Their frequent
exchange of verses must have influenced the development of
Vittoria's poetry during this period. In addition, Michelangelo
made some drawings for her: a Pietà, a Crucifixion, and
probably others as well. Their thoughts began to centre round
Christ and His passion: this became the mainspring of their
spirituality. Michelangelo's crucifixion, Vittoria thought, had
been drawn with the help of supernatural grace.[7] It represents
a crucified but living Christ—the victory of Life over Death.

Christ's body (the body of a man at his physical best) seems to symbolize the full redemption of the flesh through the Incarnation of God. There are, Vittoria says in one of her poems, two ways of gaining insight into the graces of Heaven: through the sacred writings and through the book of the Cross, and the second way is quicker and more certain. Similarly, Michelangelo, faced with temporal and eternal death, turned in his anguish towards "that Divine Love which, to take us to itself, opens its arms on the Cross"—

> *. . . a quell' amor divino,*
> *Ch'aperse a prender noi'n croce le braccia.*[8]

It was at the very time when Vittoria drew closer to Michelangelo that her friendship with Pole, who also knew the great artist,[9] began to develop. And as Vittoria had been able to transmit spiritual strength to Michelangelo, so she brought real consolation to Pole in his bereavement.[10] Her letter of condolence upon his mother's death is not extant, but we can gather from Pole's answer how much he was helped by it. It was, he wrote, the Holy Spirit Himself who had spoken through her, "that Spirit who is the fountain of all true and solid consolation, and who exercises His power then especially when we seem most destitute." In the same letter he addressed her as his second mother; already some months earlier, in a letter to Contarini, he had called her "carissimam nostram in Christo matrem" ("our dearest mother in Christ").[11]

But this was not the only relationship that existed between them. Vittoria herself was badly in need of support and turned to Pole as her chief spiritual guide. The following sonnet— evidently written before Lady Salisbury's death—is most illuminating:[12]

> *Figlio e signor, se la tua prima e vera*
> *Madre vive prigion, non l'è già tolto*
> *L'anima saggia, o 'l chiaro spirto sciolto,*
> *Nè di tante virtù l'invitta schiera.*

93

A me, che sembro andar scarca e leggiera
E'n poca terra ho il cor chiuso e sepolto,
Convien ch'abbi talor l'occhio rivolto,
Chè la novella tua madre non pèra.
Tu per gli aperti spaziosi campi
Del ciel cammini, e non più nebbia o pietra
Ritarda o ingombra il tuo spedito corso.
Io grave d'anni agghiaccio. Or tu, ch'avvampi
D' alma fiamma celeste, umil m'impetra
Dal comun Padre eterno omai soccorso.

Son and Master, though thy first and real
Mother is imprisoned, yet her prudent soul,
Her limpid spirit is not lost or bound
Nor the invincible legion of her virtues.
To me who seem unbound and unencumbered
(And yet my heart is buried in narrow soil)
To me it falls, now it is my concern
To see that thy new mother should not perish.
Travel thou through the open, spacious fields
Of Heaven—neither cloud nor rocky boulder
May hinder or retard thy speedy course.
Heavy with age, I've turned to ice; but thou
Who burn'st with heavenly flame of life, humbly
Beseech our Father for eternal help.

This is an outstanding example of Vittoria's mature poetry. The rhythm, for instance, is markedly different from the smooth monotony of much of her earlier verse. "Io grave d'anni agghiaccio": here, and indeed in the whole sonnet, the seriousness and genuine subtlety of the underlying thought are poetically realized; the intensity and the truth of the original experience are unmistakable.

"My heart is buried in narrow soil," "I've turned to ice": Vittoria was evidently going through a serious spiritual crisis. It was in fact the most serious crisis of her life. Through Valdès and some of his pupils she had been introduced to one of the most unsettling religious questions of the day: Justification, and for a time she lost all spiritual bearings.

Justification, so far from being the arid theological problem it can so easily degenerate into, is a question of the greatest practical and personal importance and was felt to be such by many of Vittoria's friends, including Contarini, Flaminio, and Pole. They felt dissatisfied with the traditional answers of the schools. How, they asked themselves anew, can any human being escape eternal death? Man is inherently and, in practice, inescapably sinful; God is just; can there be any hope for anyone? The ordinary man's answer often amounts to a naïve reliance on "good works" alone, good conduct in the widest sense of the term. But serious and sensitive Christians will always tend to be deeply impressed, or even overwhelmed, by the discrepancy between the spiritual value of such works and man's ever-mounting guilt incurred by disobedience to God. Can a man's works alone suffice to earn salvation? A considered Christian answer is bound to be in the negative; salvation cannot be *earned*. Pole went even further: the term "merit," he thought, cannot be applied to any person but Christ;[13] he and his friends echoed the humble centurion's "Lord, I am not worthy" with intense conviction and emphasis. How then can the unjust be "justified," become just in the sight of God? A possible answer is: only by faith in Him who was crucified and took upon Himself the sins of the world.

This trend of thought had of late been put forward by Luther, but it was not in a primarily Lutheran form that it was discussed in this circle. There, the basis was Valdès' teaching, embodied in particular in a little treatise with the significant title *Del Beneficio di Giesu Christo Crocifisso* (*The Benefaction of Christ Crucified*). Its author was the Augustinian monk Benedetto da Mantova; it was revised for stylistic purposes by Benedetto's friend Flaminio; and it was published in Venice in 1542, at a time when Vittoria was in close contact with Flaminio and Pole. Here is a typical passage from this work, in a contemporary English translation:[14] "What shall we say then of them that pretend and endeavour to justify themselves before God with their own law and observations? Let those persons make the comparison, and after give their judgment.

Insomuch as God will not give that honour and glory to his own law, will they then that he give it to their laws and constitutions? This honour he giveth alonely to his only-begotten Son: he only with the sacrifice of his passion hath made satisfaction for all our sins, past, present, and to come. As oft as we apply by faith this satisfaction of Christ to our souls, we obtain undoubtedly forgiveness of sins, and by his righteousness we become good and righteous before God."

Artists like Michelangelo, Vittoria, and Flaminio would be led to this conclusion mainly through their imaginative contemplation of Christ's Passion. To men like Pole the same thoughts might suggest themselves as a fruit of their intense bible-study. Ever since the early 1530's Pole had been ceaselessly studying the Scriptures. We have caught a glimpse of him lecturing to his "familia" on the Pauline Epistles; in Viterbo these studies were continued by him and his friends. The *Beneficio di Christo* itself was, of course, based on Pauline texts. The starting-point of these spiritual explorations, as so often before and since, was the Epistle to the Romans.

It had always been part of the accepted teaching of the Church that faith is necessary for justification. The point at issue was whether faith alone has a justifying effect. What, then, about works? Are they altogether useless? The *Beneficio di Christo* takes the following view: "[Justifying faith] is a work of God in us by which our old man is crucified and we become a new creature." As soon as a man is filled with this true faith "he is forthwith stirred with a most strong zeal and desire to do good works." In other words: the justified believer will do good works because he is reborn, but works performed before regeneration are of no use at all. And how is one to know whether one is justified? By the inner experience of faith. "What certainty may I have," this treatise inquires, "that my soul is united with Christ?" The answer is clear: "Certainty consisteth in true and lively faith. . . . And he that by his faith feeleth not the marvellous effects [of rebirth] . . . let him know that he hath not yet the true Christian faith" (pp. 116–34).

THE CRUCIFIXION

from a drawing by Michelangelo

THE COUNCIL OF TRENT *from an engraving by Schiavonetti*

There are two points in this teaching which must inevitably be censured by the Catholic Church: the claim to subjective certainty of justification, and the uselessness of works done before "rebirth." As to the first point, the Catholic Church teaches that the divinely founded Church dispenses divine grace in her sacraments; that the validity of these sacraments depends on objective criteria; and that the right "feeling" accompanying them is not essential to the efficacy of the Sacrament. It follows from this that, secondly, the Church cannot confine the performance of spiritually valid works to the "reborn": they simply cannot be distinguished from the unregenerate. Were it otherwise, many of the day-to-day duties prescribed by the Church would become a mere mockery to those who have not been singled out for justification. The Church must refuse to discriminate and must treat all her children as potentially justified, leaving the ultimate sifting to another Judge.

The full Catholic answers to all these difficult questions have been quite clear since the Council of Trent, but they were not so clear before. In addition, it must be realized that the members of the Viterbo circle were not trained theologians, and these are obviously matters for theologians. Pole, the chief guide of this group, had never made good his earlier neglect of theology. True, he had read the Scriptures very attentively, and he seems to have studied some of the Fathers (particularly Augustine). But post-patristic theology, particularly the teaching of the great medieval schoolmen, was virtually unknown to him. He had taken Sadoleto's warning against the voluminous, quarrelsome books of the scholastics all too seriously. These theological subtleties and distinctions, he must have thought, were they not merely the "wisdom of the world" and therefore "foolishness with God"? Was there anything that mattered except the preaching of "Christ crucified"?

This comes out very clearly in an unpublished reform treatise of Pole's. At first, he writes, God revealed His mysteries in a book given to all nations: the book of heaven and earth. But men, in their pride and folly, did not understand this law and would have been eternally lost if God, in His infinite mercy, had not given them a second book, "the book of the Cross of Jesus Christ, the contents of which are more absurd, more remote from human wisdom than anything that can be said or thought" ("liber crucis Jesu Christi ea continens, quibus absurdius nihil, nihil ab humana sapientia remotius dici aut cogitari posse videtur").[15] "The book of the Cross": these are the very words used by Vittoria, and here they are given a definitely anti-rational meaning. Pole sometimes tended to underestimate the rational basis of faith or even to treat reason and faith as mutually exclusive. Pole did not pursue these thoughts to their logical conclusions, but it is obvious enough that the kind of mystical contemplation of the Cross practised by him and his friends could easily encourage a certain vagueness of belief. Even if the members of the Pole circle did not accept the whole doctrine of the *Beneficio di Christo*, they were certainly not well equipped for perceiving its dangers. The current theology of the day, on the other hand, was not vigorous enough to satisfy the legitimate religious needs of Pole and his friends—hence their attempt to express these matters in terms nearer to their own lives.

Behind this doctrinal groping in the dark, it must be remembered, was much personal conflict and anxiety. Vittoria, in a letter to a friend, described her spiritual troubles in the following terms: "You have witnessed the chaos of ignorance in which I was, the labyrinth of errors in which I wandered, . . . my body perpetually in movement to find repose and my soul ever agitated in its search for peace."[16] Further insight into her crisis comes from Carnesecchi: "Before the Marchesa," he reports, "contracted her friendship with the Cardinal [Pole], she used to afflict herself so much with fasts, sackcloth, and other mortifications of the flesh that she had reduced herself to skin and bone, and this she did, perhaps, because she placed too much confidence in such works, imagining that true piety and religion, and consequently the salvation of one's soul, consisted in these things. But after being advised by the Cardinal that she rather offended God than the reverse by treating her body with such austerity and rigour . . . she began to desist from that very austere mode of life, reducing her mortifications little by little to a just and reasonable mean."[17] It seems that Vittoria's spiritual conflict had reached its climax when she joined Pole in Viterbo, for only just over two months later she wrote to a friend: "I owe the health both of my soul and of my body to Cardinal Pole; the former was endangered by superstition, the latter by misrule."[18]

Pole not only helped her to reduce her mortifications to a "just and reasonable mean"; he also restrained her restless probing into doctrinal problems. Pole's attitude was eminently reasonable. We are told that he admonished her several times not to be too curious and not to overstep the limits set to the human mind.[19] At the same time he tried to satisfy her spiritual needs by his religious discourses. These made an indelible impression on Vittoria's mind. Here is her description of them in her only letter to Pole that seems to have survived: "Whenever you speak of the most wonderful sacrifice, of our eternal destination, of the love that flows out towards us, . . . whenever you pierce with the sword of the word all our [undue] confidence, then my soul is given wings and feels sure of reaching the desired nest."[20] "Thou," she had written earlier, "who burn'st with heavenly flame of life": now that flame was giving her the longed-for light and warmth.

"Piercing all our undue confidence": this suggests Pole's advice about the works of mortification, in which Vittoria had evidently placed much confidence. For the rest, Pole was unable to produce a theological formula that would have set her mind at rest. The solution which he proposed to her was perhaps not unworthy of an Englishman: he advised her to *believe* that she could only be saved by faith, but to *act* as if she could only be saved by works.[21] At first sight this may look like an evasion of the main difficulty, but in reality it is an intelligible and practical answer, implying a healthy awareness of the mystery of things. Pole's advice on this crucial matter is confirmed by his general attitude to the difficulties which any interpretation of the Pauline epistles must be prepared to face. When he was consulted, we are told, "by what method the hidden and obscure passages of St. Paul's epistles might be unfolded and brought to light, he used to make the following answer: that the most ready and expeditious way he could propose, was for the reader to begin at the latter part of the epistles, where the apostle treats of morality, and to practise what was delivered there; and then go back to the beginning, where the doctrinal parts are reasoned on with great acuteness and subtlety."[22] Similarly, Flaminio recommended *The Imitation of Christ* more than any other book except the Bible; it should be read, he suggested, "not out of curiosity or in order to reason and dispute about Christian things," but in order to attain "to the practice of a Christian life."[23] Pole and Flaminio, without attaining perfect clarity in their minds, were certainly not in danger of following Luther in his radical disparagement of the human will; in an important sense they were, and remained, Erasmians.

It has of course been suggested time and again that the members of the Viterbo circle (the "spirituali," as they were called by some contemporaries) were really "Protestants" without knowing it themselves. Such statements appear to rest on a misunderstanding. The "spirituali," it is true, showed some affinity with Luther's view on justification. But it is equally important to remember that, with the exception of Carnesecchi, they never adopted any Protestant doctrines on the Eucharist, let alone on the Church. Pole, for example, is known to have felt great love and reverence for the Sacrament of the Altar, and the attitude of the "spirituali" to their Church was most concisely expressed by Flaminio in 1543: "We wish . . . on no account, however cogent the reasons may appear, to allow ourselves to be separated from the unity of the Catholic Church."[24] It would be difficult to think of a more "un-Protestant" statement than this.

The "spirituali" were, however, painfully and anxiously

aware of the religious cleavage in Christendom. But was the breach quite beyond repair? In June 1537, when Pole and Contarini were earnestly studying the Lutheran Confession of Augsburg, Pole had expressed his opinion that a reunion of all Christians could easily be brought about.[25] This optimism was shared by Contarini. The friends must have rejoiced when, for a brief moment in 1541, it seemed that their hopes would come true.

In that year, a religious colloquy was held in Ratisbon between Catholic and Protestant representatives, in the presence of the Emperor Charles V, whose policy, at that particular moment, required an amicable settlement of the German schism. The chief Catholic representative was Cardinal Contarini. The appointment of the leading Church reformer to this post was of great significance; no other member of the College of Cardinals was so qualified for this task as Contarini. Some years before he had concluded a treatise against the Lutherans with these moving words: "If we wish to put an end to the Lutheran errors and troubles we need not muster against them heaps of books, Ciceronian orations, or subtle arguments: let us rely on the probity of our lives and a humble spirit, desiring nothing but the good of Christ and our neighbours."[26] And now he wrote in a similar vein to the redoubtable Catholic controversialist Dr. Eck: "It is our duty to continue steadfast in prayer to the God of peace and unity, that He may send down His Holy Spirit from heaven into our hearts and restore the unity of His Church. Therefore I believe it is our part to strive, by goodwill and well-doing, to put our opponents to shame or bring them to think shame of themselves for separating from brethren who are filled with love."[27] Contarini was not likely to forget that Christian schismatics and heretics remained his "fratres," even though they were "fratres separati."

When the negotiations started in earnest, towards the end of April 1541, it was found, to Contarini's great delight, that real progress could be made in the question of justification by faith. The basis of the attempted compromise was a formula worked out by one of Contarini's colleagues and whole-heartedly accepted by Contarini himself. The formula spoke of a twofold justification ("duplex iustitia"). Inspired by the Holy Ghost, man becomes aware of sin, turns to God, and acquires a "iustitia inhaerens." This, however, is imperfect and is supplemented by an entirely unmerited "iustitia imputata"—a justification imputed to him through faith in Christ's perfect sacrifice on the Cross. This formula does not avoid the usual pitfalls of a compromise: it disregards some of the outstanding difficulties (e.g. subjective certainty of Justification and Free Will). Though it was to have its vigorous adherents at Trent it was not adopted by the Council, which produced a clearer and more comprehensive decision. At Ratisbon, however, it had the satisfactory effect of pleasing the Protestant theologians, led by Melanchthon, owing to the inclusion of the word "imputed." Contarini, for his part, was sincerely convinced that the formula did not run counter to Catholic teaching, as indeed it can hardly be said to have done before the Tridentine decrees. Pole shared Contarini's belief to the full. In a letter to Contarini he likened the formula to a partly concealed pearl, always possessed by the Church, but now accessible to everyone.[28]

The initial success of the Ratisbon colloquy was destined to be short-lived. Church discipline, invocation of saints, the Eucharist, the Mass, celibacy, the monastic life—all these points produced violent dissension, not to mention two other questions (Council and Papal Supremacy) which had been shelved for the time being. On 22 May, after barely a month, the negotiations were abandoned. Meanwhile, Luther himself had sent a letter of disapproval, and the Protestant princes would certainly not have felt themselves bound by any decision that endangered their political schemes. Nor had Rome yet spoken. Some of the Cardinals disliked the formula on justification; the Pope himself, following his usual practice, did not let anybody know what he thought. It was evidently too late for a reunion: too many interests were thriving on the schism, and the mental gulf between Protestants and Catholics had become very wide indeed. The breakdown of these negotiations has lain heavily on Christendom ever since.

One gulf had just proved unbridgeable. Another was about to open, and that as a direct consequence of Contarini's failure. The methods adopted to restore Christian unity had aroused the intense suspicion of men like Caraffa (of Caraffa specially, but he had his staunch adherents in the College of Cardinals and beyond). These men had noticed, for instance, that Sadoleto had gone out of his way to win back Calvin's Genevan congregation by sending them a most conciliatory letter. Both Sadoleto and Contarini had used their influence to prevent any severe action against Italians of doubtful orthodoxy; again and again they and their friends had recommended patience and gentle persuasion. Pole, too, had shown conspicuous leniency in Viterbo; he had supported Contarini's formula and had consorted with suspects like Carnesecchi and Flaminio. All this was sufficient evidence for a man of Caraffa's martial temperament. He jumped to the conclusion that the "spirituali" and all their friends were nothing but disguised heretics.

In August 1542 Caraffa's suspicions were considerably strengthened by a scandal of the first order: the apostasy of the two religious, Peter Martyr (Vermigli) and Bernardino Ochino, the best-known disciples of Juan de Valdès. Both of them had been intimately connected with the "spirituali." When Peter Martyr had got into trouble with the authorities, Contarini had come to his rescue; Ochino, the General of the Capuchins, had always enjoyed the special protection of Vittoria Colonna. Like most of his friends, Ochino had meditated much on justification, but unlike them he had come to adopt the full Lutheran answer to this question. It seems that he arrived at his position some time in 1540 or thereabouts. This was not at first realized by the enthusiastic crowds that flocked to his sermons, but the development of his views was watched with increasing suspicion by some circles in Rome. At length, on 15 July 1542, he received a courteously worded invitation to come to Rome. Only six days later the Pope issued the bull "Licet ab initio," which established the Roman Inquisition, under the leadership of Caraffa. Ochino, at that moment in Verona, was in no hurry to obey the summons. A papal brief of 27 July renewed the invitation and ordered him to start without delay. Thereupon he set out on his journey southwards. In Florence he met Peter Martyr who had also been cited to Rome and had decided to go into exile. Ochino's mind was in turmoil, and in his anguish he wrote a letter to Vittoria Colonna, dated 22 August. "I find myself here," he wrote, "in no small trouble of mind, having come here with the intention of going to Rome, although many people dissuaded me from doing so before I arrived. But, understanding better every day the way things are going on, I am most particularly persuaded by Peter Martyr and others not to go; because I could not but deny Christ or be crucified. The first I will not do; the second, yes, but with His grace, and when it shall be His will. I have not now the spirit to go voluntarily to death. When God requires me, He will know to find me anywhere. . . . After this, what could I do more in Italy? . . . On the other hand, think if it is not hard for me in all respects! I know you will think so. The flesh recoils from leaving everything behind and thinking what will be said. It would be more than welcome to me to speak with you, and to have your opinion and that of the reverend Monsignor Pole, or to have a letter from you. Pray to Our Lord for me; I desire more than ever to serve Him with His Grace. Salute everybody."[29] On the following day he took to flight. Two days later Peter Martyr followed him.

The sensation was immense. For the Viterbo circle the grief of these days was made all the more poignant by Contarini's sudden death on 24 August, the day after Ochino's flight. In a letter of condolence to Contarini's sister, Vittoria wrote: "Now no other spiritual service remains to me than that of the most illustrious and most reverend Monsignor of England, his singular, intimate, and most true friend, and more than son and brother, who feels this loss so much that his strong pious mind, unvanquished by so many varied troubles, seems to have given itself over to grief more than it has done on any other occasion."[30]

Vittoria proved her willingness to submit to Pole's spiritual direction when Ochino, a short time after his flight, sent her a book of his in order to justify himself in her eyes. Pole advised her to send the book to Cardinal Cervini in Rome, and this she did at once. She was, in fact, very careful to dissociate herself from the apostate who, as she put it to Cervini, had placed himself outside the "ark of salvation."[31] Though there was no reason to doubt her sincerity, the Inquisitors remained unconvinced. Both she and Pole were at the moment beyond their reach, but in the secret inquisitorial records the Viterbo "spirituali" were always referred to as plain heretics.[32] Some years later, Caraffa was to have an opportunity to bring his charges against Pole into the open. Meanwhile he devoted himself with great enthusiasm to the work of the Inquisition. "Without waiting for a financial grant from the Camera Apostolica, he fitted up a house at his own expense as a place where the Inquisition might hold its sessions."[33] The heresy-hunt was up.

It was by no means easy to decide how the Church should deal with men who deliberately flouted her authority. Not long afterwards Pole himself was to have this problem thrust upon him on an unexpected and frightening scale. But the fact remains that his general attitude to it, as to so much else, turned out to be very different from Caraffa's. The differences were so great that Pole and Caraffa, fellow-workers in the field of Church reform, ceased to be able to understand each other's language. Doctrinal disagreements, practical divergences, differences of temperament: all these the accommodating and urbane Pole could have accepted without much difficulty. But more than this was involved. Pole continued to represent Catholic Reform; Caraffa was the first leader of the Counter-Reformation.

NOTES TO CHAPTER SIX

[1] Most of this paragraph is based on Beccadelli's Life (*Q.*, vol. v). I have not been able to see G. Signorelli, *Viterbo nella storia della Chiesa* (Viterbo, 1940), which may contain some more details about Pole's life in Viterbo.

[2] *Q.*, vol. v, p. 387.

[3] *Q.*, vol. iii, p. 42.

[4] Cf. Estratto del Processo di Pietro Carnesecchi (ed. G. Manzoni, *Miscellanea di Storia Italiana*, Tomo x, 1870), p. 254. For Bartholomeo Stella, cf. Cistellini, *Figure della Riforma Pretridentina* (1948).

[5] Francisco de Hollanda, *Vier Gespräche über die Malerei* (ed. de Vasconcellos, 1899), p. 31.

[6] *Rime e Lettere di Michelagnolo Buonarotti* (Firenze, 1892), p. 340 ("Poscia ch' appreso ha l'arte intera e diva").

[7] Vittoria Colonna, *Carteggio* (ed. Ferrero and Müller, 1889), p. 209. Cf. illustration facing p. 144.

[8] Vittoria Colonna, *Rime e Lettere* (Firenze, 1860), p. 336; Michelangelo, op. cit., p. 339 ("Giunto e già 'l corso della vita mia").

[9] Condivi's Life (Michelangelo, op. cit., p. 145). Pole possessed a drawing by Michelangelo, representing a Pietà (M. Haile, *Life of Pole*, p. 323).

[10] For their relationship, cf. H. Jedin in *L'Italia Francescana* (1947), vol. xxii, pp. 13–30.

[11] *Q.*, vol. iii, p. 78; vol. iii, p. 14 (4th February, 1541).

[12] Vittoria Colonna, *Rime e Lettere* (Firenze, 1860), p. 358. This editor entitles the poem "In Morte del Marchese del Vasto," but older editions do not contain this title, nor do I see any reason to accept it. I conclude from internal evidence that this sonnet is addressed to Pole. Mgr. Dr. H. Jedin, of Rome, whom I have asked for advice on this matter, has kindly let me know that he regards this conclusion as almost certainly correct. It may not be irrelevant to add that in the Bergamo edition of 1760 the preceding sonnet contains a pun on "'l divin Polo" (pole-star and Pole). (This sonnet, incidentally, is not addressed to Vittoria's brother Federigo who died in 1516, but to Cardinal Federigo Fregoso, a friend and collaborator of Pole's. A critical edition of Vittoria's works is badly needed.)

[13] Processo Carnesecchi, op. cit., p. 550.

[14] *The Benefit of Christ's Death*, ed. C. Babington (1855), pp. 108 seq. The translation was made in 1548 by Pole's kinsman Edward Courtenay, the son of the Marquis of Exeter.

[15] MSS. *Vat. Lat.* 5964, fols. 114a, b, 115b (Vatican Library). This treatise contains copious quotations from St. Paul. In Pole's published writings, too, there are hardly any quotations from books other than the Scriptures and the Fathers. Cf. *Q.*, vol. v, p. 390.

[16] To Cardinal Morone, 22 December 1543: Vittoria Colonna, *Carteggio*, p. 273.

[17] Processo Carnesecchi, op. cit., p. 499 (I follow the translation in M. Jerrold, *Vittoria Colonna* (1906), pp, 276–7).

[18] To Giulia Gonzaga: Colonna, *Carteggio*, p. 238.

[19] Processo Carnesecchi, op. cit., p. 503.

[20] Colonna, *Carteggio*, p. 264 (15 July 1543).

[21] Processo Carnesecchi, op. cit., p. 269.

[22] T. Phillips, *Life of Pole*, vol. ii, p. 288, quoting Cardinal Seripando.

[23] Letter to Gualteruzzi, 28 February 1542: *Q.*, vol. iii, Preface, p. 69.

24 Pastor, *History of the Popes*, vol. xi, p. 485. On Pole's reverence for the Sacrament of the Altar, see *Q.*, vol. v, p. 340; *S.P. Ven.*, vol. vi, part 3, No. 1292.

25 *Q.*, vol. ii, p. 68.

26 Contarini, *Opera* (1571), p. 580.

27 F. Dittrich, *Regesten und Briefe des Kardinals Gasparo Contarini* (1881), p. 315. (Pastor, op. cit., vol. xi, pp. 433–4).

28 16th July 1541: *Q.*, vol. iii, p. 30.

29 Colonna, *Carteggio*, pp. 247 seq. (Translation from Jerrold, op. cit., pp. 256–7.)

30 Colonna, *Carteggio*, p. 251. (Jerrold, op. cit., p. 266.)

31 Colonna, *Carteggio*, p. 257 (4th December, 1542).

32 E.g., "Compendium processuum Sancti Officii," ed. Corvisieri, *Archivio della Società romana di storia patria* (1880), vol. iii, p. 279. Cf. also Processo Carnesecchi, *passim*.

33 Pastor, op. cit., vol. xii, p. 507.

CHAPTER SEVEN

COUNCIL AND CONCLAVE
(1545–1553)

DURING his time in Viterbo Pole was entering on the second stage of his spiritual maturity. Naturally diffident and developing late, he had willingly submitted to the guidance of Contarini, the "Venetian Thomas More."[1] Now others began to lean on Pole as their "duca, signore, e maestro." It was in this capacity, more than in any other, that he imprinted himself on the minds of some of the best among his contemporaries. He preserved the gifted Flaminio from losing himself in over-intense religious speculations; he restored Vittoria Colonna's peace of mind; and there were many others who learnt much from this outstanding teacher. (Michelangelo, for example, derived profit from Pole's "virtuous and learned discourse."[2]) Pole himself had been thoroughly "ploughed up"; he had died with Thomas More and again with his mother. "Whosoever shall lose his life, shall save it": he had experienced this life-giving death, and this alone enabled him to transmit new life to his disciples. Meanwhile he did not forget his and Contarini's wider concern to transmit new life to the whole Church. Hopes had run high at the time of the bold "Consilium de Emendanda Ecclesia" (1537), when Contarini had written to Pole: "Almost all the Cardinals favour reform . . . I cherish a great hope that our cause will prosper from day to day."[3] Many days had passed since then: what was the position at the time of Contarini's death (1542)?

Contarini's hopes had been disappointed, despite the unceasing efforts of himself and his friends, including Caraffa and Pole. These Catholic reformers soon discovered that not nearly so many Cardinals as Contarini had thought were in favour of reform. If the indictment contained in the "Consilium" was true (and that was not seriously denied by anybody) the utmost speed was called for in reforming the Church of God. But the reformers had to wrestle with Cardinals who had been raised to the purple by worldly Popes and had no ambition to outshine their former masters. Though often paying lip-service to the now fashionable creed of reform, they were determined to postpone what seemed to them the deluge until after their deaths.

In this not altogether surprising situation everything turned on the attitude of the reigning Pope. Paul III, it is true, had initiated the reform proceedings. Now and again he was prepared to make another move in that direction, but only now and again. He stands, as Pastor has indicated, at the parting of the ways: laying the foundations of Catholic reform, yet in some respects continuing the evil line of Renaissance Popes. The luxury and brilliance of his court was reminiscent of the times of Leo X; it was even more serious that he involved the Papacy in the affairs of his family, the Farnese, and practised unlimited nepotism. He was, after all, an older contemporary of Leo X, and no thoroughgoing change could be expected in a man who was sixty-seven when he ascended the Papal throne. Titian's picture shows him as he was: a highly intelligent, wily old man. He spoke little and all his words were carefully chosen. He listened all the more and his eventual decision usually tried to combine all the different views suggested to him. This habit, admirable in a conservative ruler, did not mark him out as a consistent reformer. Again and again he shelved a necessary decree or unduly delayed its preparation.

Contarini was sometimes not far from despair. Just then, sure enough, the Pope would revive his hopes. "Our good old man," Contarini wrote to Pole on one of these occasions, "spoke to me privately about reform, in a way which made me again conceive great hopes."[4] But afterwards the "good old man" would draw back again. On such a crucial and simple matter, for example, as the episcopal duty of residence the Pope failed to take decisive action. He tried to persuade the bishops who lived in Rome (eighty of them) to go back to their flocks; he even set them a time-limit for complying with this request. When nothing happened he had a bull drawn up. That alone took nearly a year. Finally, when the bull was ready, its publication was indefinitely deferred.

All this must not be taken to mean that no progress at all was made under Paul III. We have mentioned in a preceding chapter (Chapter 4) that Paul III began to reform the morals of the Roman clergy, and there is evidence that this had a measure of success. He also took steps to reform the curial offices. Pole was a member of the commission for the reform of the Apostolic Camera (the Papal Exchequer), and in 1542 an appropriate decree was issued and put into execution. Residence of bishops, too, though not yet legally enforced, tended to become more frequent. Contarini himself, in June 1541, admitted that many abuses had come to an end.[5]

Much, clearly, would depend on the future of a renewal of the corrupt College of Cardinals. Here again Paul III showed his temporizing nature. It is quite true and very remarkable that he promoted some excellent men entirely on their merits. Contarini, Pole, Sadoleto, Caraffa, Cortese are the outstanding examples. But he also raised very different men to the purple: the pleasure-loving del Monte, some prelates of evil repute, and one of his own nephews at the ripe age of fourteen. More seriously still, practically all the cardinals created in 1538 were nominated by the Emperor or the King of France; thus, the inherited cleavage in the Sacred College between Imperialists and adherents of France, reflecting the chief European rivalry between France and Spain, was fatefully continued. On this occasion one Cardinal was reserved "in petto" in the interests of Venice. He was proclaimed a little later and turned out to be none other than the epicurean Pietro Bembo.[6]

This promotion, much discussed then and later, was presumably meant as a friendly gesture towards the Italian literary coterie and it may have had its effect in silencing potential criticism from that quarter; even the obscene rogue Aretino now discovered his latent sense of religion and began to hope for the purple. Bembo, to be sure, was not a second Aretino, and it may well be that in later life his outlook became more serious, but that should not have sufficed to gain him a cardinal's hat. He took no part in any reform work and administered the Italian diocese entrusted to him mostly from a safe distance. His elevation remains an absurdity.

These mistakes would have been less serious if Paul III had succeeded in convening a General Council during the early years of his reign. In this field, more than in any other, the Pope could justly lay some part of the blame on the two warring monarchs, Charles V and Francis I. Once again, the interests of the secular rulers proved to be at variance with the interests of religion; Paul III, on the other hand, was not sufficiently single-minded to rescue the Papacy from its prolonged and profound implication in the "cares of the world that choke the Word."

A Council was convoked to meet at Mantua in 1537, three years after Paul's accession, and again at Vicenza in the following year. Neither meeting came to anything. In 1542 a Council was convoked at Trent, an Italian city just within the borders of the Empire, and three Papal legates, among them Pole, were sent there to open it. Hardly anybody else appeared. The legates waited for six months, until the Pope recalled them from this ignominious position. On each occasion the futile wars between Charles and Francis, or the tangled diplomacy accompanying them, caused the loss of valuable time. It was not until December 1545 that the Council was opened at Trent, but even then the initial attendance was small: five cardinals, four archbishops, twenty-six bishops, three abbots, and five generals of Orders (among the latter the great Augustinian Seripando). Pole was again one of the three Papal legates named to preside over the Council. Pole's journey from Viterbo to Trent was far from easy, for he had to evade the

assassins sent by Henry VIII; on this occasion the King went
to the length of hiring some well-known Italian condottieri
with their retinue. Pole therefore travelled by a devious route
with an armed escort of twenty-five horsemen, while one of
his 'servants, disguised as a cardinal, acted as a decoy along
the usual road.[7]

The Council had been held up for over eight years mainly
owing to political reasons. When it did meet in 1545 it was of
course regarded by many as primarily a political event. The
Bishop of Trent was virtually an Imperial representative, and
the French bishops were not remiss in looking after their King's
interests. This was not exactly what Pole and his friends had
hoped for. In a treatise, *De Concilio*, written before his journey to
Trent, Pole made some powerful comments on the interference of
secular rulers in the business of a General Council. Were these
rulers, he asked, the right persons to influence religious affairs?
Rich men, it was known, would find it difficult to enter into the
kingdom of God; to do so would be far more difficult for
secular rulers who were usually puffed up with riches, honours,
and worldly pleasures of all kinds. What mattered now was
not pomp and secular interests, but a humble and repentant
heart determined to confess the common guilt of Christendom
and to make amends.[8]

To write like this in a treatise destined for private circulation
is one thing: to state it publicly is quite another. Yet it was just
such an outspoken statement that Pole drew up for the Second
Session of the Council, on 7 January 1546. Here are some
relevant passages from this remarkable document: "Before the
tribunal of God's mercy we, the shepherds, should make ourselves responsible for all the evils now burdening the flock of
Christ. . . . It will be found that it is our ambition, our avarice,
our cupidity which have wrought all these evils on the people of
God, and that it is because of these sins that shepherds are being
driven from their churches, and the churches starved of the Word
of God, and the property of the Church, which is the property
of the poor, stolen, and the priesthood given to the unworthy

and to men who differ from lay-folk only in dress. If God punished us as we deserved, we should long since have been as Sodom and Gomorrah."

Plain speaking of this kind must have surprised the Fathers of the Council who had probably expected a conventional opening speech saturated with inoffensive piety (they all turned their faces towards Pole as soon as the secretary of the Council had read the first sentences of this statement). But Pole had not yet done with them. He went on to implore them not to be swayed in their deliberations by anger, hatred, or friendship. "All classes of men," he wrote, "are prone to this, and those especially who serve princes. They easily speak for love or for hate, according as they think their princes are affected, from whom they await reward. . . . We therefore admonish the delegates that they serve their princes with all loyalty and zeal; but as becomes bishops. They must serve them as the servants of God and not as servants of men. . . . Our struggle is not only with flesh and blood but with 'spiritual wickedness in the high places.'"[9] "The King's good servant but God's first": Thomas More's last message, confirmed by much bitter experience in the intervening ten years, was the gist of this burning exhortation.

Pole took a considerable part in the early business of the Council. On one occasion his intervention was specially important, when it was debated whether tradition should be regarded as a source of belief as well as Scripture. Though Pole was an assiduous Bible student, he refused to take his stand on the Bible alone and carried the majority with him on this point. This was decided in April 1546. Then followed a series of reform discussions, and in June the debate was opened on the great dogmatic question of the day: Justification. This debate went on for a long time and resulted in a comprehensive decree on justification published several months later.

Meanwhile Pole's health had broken down, and he left the Council for Padua at the end of June 1546. This departure at the very time when justification began to be discussed gave rise to unpleasant rumours at the time, and the suspicion of a "diplomatic illness" has been frequently repeated since, even by Ranke. This suspicion is quite unfounded. Pole, in fact, continued to take part in the Council by means of letters and memoranda; moreover, his views on justification were ably and persistently represented by Seripando.[10] The opinion of Pole and Seripando amounted to a restatement of Contarini's Ratisbon formula about twofold justification—inherent and imputed. This formula was given prolonged and sometimes heated consideration (on one occasion a bishop even violently took a colleague by the beard) and was finally rejected. Instead, a decree was drawn up which represented the best that the theologians of the Catholic Reform could produce, and that best was very good indeed. Any student of this decree is bound to feel that it deals conscientiously with a very difficult question and that it arrives at a balanced conclusion. Only a combination of faith and works, it teaches, can justify; man is not entirely powerless either to resist grace or to co-operate with it. The decree also clarifies the all-important issue of subjective certainty of justification; no man, it states, can be certain that he is justified. The tenth chapter introduces a new and particularly helpful point: justification is not regarded as something that, happening once, happens once for all. On the one hand, a justified man may fall and be again justified; on the other hand, man's justification may deepen with his fidelity in the passing years. There is evidence that Pole, who was ready enough to learn from others, saw the merits of this decree and accepted it, not only out of obedience to the Church, but because his mind was genuinely convinced.[11]

The Pope had allowed Pole to leave Trent and was considerate enough not to insist on his return in a state of ill-health. In any case, the Council was virtually suspended early in the following year, owing to a political quarrel between Pope and Emperor. The decree on justification was destined to remain its only major achievement for some years.

Pole's ill-health, followed by the suspension of the Council, may have contained a personal message for him. A comparison between his best-known portrait (by Sebastiano del Piombo) and later likenesses suggests that he must have aged very rapidly. Other reminders of mortality came through the deaths of his friends: Contarini in 1542, Giberti in 1543, Sadoleto in 1547, and in the same year his second mother Vittoria Colonna, after a painful illness. All these friends had been Pole's seniors, but in 1550 even Flaminio, almost exactly his contemporary, died. The shadows were lengthening.

At that very moment when the decline was beginning it seemed as if Pole's life was about to take an entirely new turn. Paul III died on 10 November 1549, and by the end of the month it seemed practically certain that Pole would become his successor. The Conclave which was to elect the new Pope lasted for nearly three months; it was one of the major experiences of Pole's life and it must therefore be described in some detail.

A few years later Pole referred to this Conclave as "that comedy, not to say tragedy" ("illam comoediam ne dicam tragoediam").[12] Let us first look at the comic side of the proceedings.[13] The word "conclave" denotes an assembly behind locked doors. Nothing could have been further from the truth in this case. Or rather, the doors were indeed locked, but openings were made in the walls, and one ambassador climbed with ladders over roofs in order to speak with a cardinal. Moreover, there was constant coming and going among the numerous personal servants of the cardinals. These "conclavists" saw to it that the connection between their masters and the outer world was not interrupted. The slightest change in any of the candidates' chances was reported to the Roman bankers' shops, where the betting was in full swing from the very day of the old Pope's death; the "conclavists" themselves went partners with the bankers in this lucrative business.[14]

Meanwhile, the cardinals did everything in their power to defeat the austerity regulations prescribed for a Conclave. They were housed in the largest halls of the Vatican, including the Sistine Chapel overlooked by Michelangelo's lately finished

Last Judgment, and each cardinal was supposed to occupy a simple wooden cell erected for this purpose. Instead, some cardinals enlarged their cells by means of special structures in front, and others annexed the empty cells of absent members. And some of them were indeed in need of space, having brought their barbers and cooks with them. Disregarding all rules about fasting, the cardinals invited each other to gargantuan feasts. Most of them being Southerners by birth and temperament, there were many wordy encounters and exciting scenes. The place swarmed with human beings (about 350 of them), and after a time things began to be far less pleasant than in the beginning, the atmosphere growing intolerably foul from the fumes of candles and the stench of lavatories. After two months the Venetian ambassador had to report: "The greater part of those who leave the Conclave depart sick and almost dead. . . . The stench is so great that the first physician in Rome, having entered the Conclave, threatened them with the plague on this account."[15]

Why then did the cardinals continue the Conclave when it became so unpleasant? The answer is simple enough: because most of them were agents of one of the great secular powers (Spain under the Emperor Charles V and France). This was in fact the chief tragic aspect of this costly farce. It was the inevitable outcome of Paul III's political promotions. There were two clear-cut and evenly divided parties among the cardinals: adherents of the Emperor and adherents of France, and hardly any neutrals. At the very beginning of the election the Emperor drew up a list of his candidates and of those he wished to exclude at all costs. Among the Emperor's chief candidates was Pole (who, at about this time, was awarded a pension from Imperial funds).[16] The reasons for this choice are obscure. The Emperor may have believed that Pole's stand for Katherine of Aragon would ensure his allegiance to the Spanish side, or perhaps he thought him a political simpleton and as such an easy prey. Be that as it may, the fact remains that Pole's chances of obtaining the Papacy depended entirely on the Emperor's back-

ing. Pole was generally regarded as superior to the other cardinals in "nobility, goodness, and doctrine,"[17] but this superiority was, in fact, an obstacle, because the worldly majority
among the cardinals were afraid of Pole's reforming zeal. "They
consider it certain," wrote a shrewd observer, "that [in case of
Pole's election] the whole of this Court would have to lead a
new life";[18] this prospect they contemplated with horror.

As an Imperial candidate, however, Pole could always count
on some twenty votes; he received twenty-one on 3 December, and twenty-four on the following day. As most of the
French cardinals had not yet arrived, there were only forty-one
cardinals present, and the necessary majority of two-thirds
was therefore twenty-eight. In the evening of 4 December
the French ambassador came to the door of the Conclave and
announced that the French cardinals had already reached
Corsica and would arrive soon (in fact he had no idea where
they actually were). Thereupon the Imperialist cardinals
decided to act at once. That very night they made preparations
for an unusual but probably lawful mode of election: the acclama-
tion of Pole by a general rendering of homage ("per adora-
tionem"). It seems that they succeeded in persuading a
sufficient number of cardinals that this course should be followed.
Two of them went to Pole's cell to fetch him for the ceremony,
but they met with an unexpected refusal. Pole told them that
he wished to enter the Papacy through the door, not through
the window; in full daylight, not under cover of darkness.[19]

Though this plan had miscarried, the Imperialists were confident that Pole would be elected in the usual way on the
following day, 5 December. They had all the more reason
to expect this as they had received the promise from three
wavering cardinals to support Pole if the latter received
twenty-six votes. The Roman bookmakers, too, were quite
sure that Pole would be made Pope that morning.[20] The
cardinals packed up their belongings ready to leave the
Vatican; the papal vestments were laid out; outside, the people
began to assemble for the blessing by the new Pope. At the

ballot Pole received twenty-three votes. Then two more cardinals rose and transferred their votes to him (such subsequent accessions were customary). Pole had now twenty-five votes. One more, and the three waverers would add their votes and complete the election. Deep silence followed, broken after a while by the Cardinal-Dean who asked if there were any more accessions to Pole's side. No response. Then the Dean concluded the meeting and the cardinals dispersed, after another unsuccessful ballot. Pole had not been elected, to everyone's astonishment. A few days later the French cardinals arrived and put an end to Pole's chances; as an Imperial candidate Pole was of course unacceptable to the French King.

In the end, after long haggling, the two parties compromised by electing Cardinal del Monte (Julius III), a worldly man who loved his ease. From the point of view of Church reform, this choice was indeed "tragic." In addition, Pole must have been deeply hurt by what he described as the "mutual recriminations and false calumnies" among the cardinals. Some of the calumnies were directed against himself. He had not hitherto been aware of Caraffa's deep-seated suspicion of the "spirituali"; now he was suddenly exposed to a violent attack from Caraffa who openly accused him of heretical leanings. It was not difficult for Pole to clear himself in the eyes of the cardinals, but it was a painful and ominous experience. "Among my friends," Pole wrote some years later, "Cardinal Caraffa was pre-eminent for age and rank. That he should be torn from me by the artifices of Satan . . . was a blow that I could not help lamenting bitterly."[21]

What was going on in Pole's mind during this conclave which brought him so near to the Papal throne? We can gather something from a letter he wrote to a Spanish friend in June 1550, only a few months after the end of the Conclave.[22] In this very personal letter he tried to find out the true significance for his life of this strange sequence of events. Had he perhaps failed in his duty, when he refused the "adoration" of the cardinals that night? Had he, once again, been deaf to the call of "vita activa"? But then, was he really cut out for a Pope? Was that the part ("persona," as he called it) assigned to him by God? What, in fact, was his part on the stage of life?

Some of his friends, he writes, had praised his behaviour during the Conclave as showing greatness of mind and fortitude. He himself was of the opinion that those who accused him of pusillanimity and indolence were far less wrong. He admitted that he had been alarmed by the burden of the Papacy. Had he therefore refused to canvass the Cardinals on his own behalf? Not altogether, perhaps. He had in fact not been clear in his own mind whether God meant him to be Pope. This was the thing that mattered most: to find out God's will and then not to resist it. On reflection it seemed to him that throughout his life God had meant him to play the part of an ordinary beast of burden. Yes, the metaphor was perfectly correct: like a beast of burden he was sullen and devoid of a sense of honour, but ready to perform the tasks imposed by his master. That night, when the two Cardinals came to fetch him for the "adoration," he thought for a moment that he was like that ass which Christ sent the apostles to loose and bring to Him, that He, seated on it, might enter the Holy City. But then he grew afraid of the darkness and asked them to postpone the election until the dawn. The dramatic ballot next morning showed that he had been right in his refusal: Christ evidently had no need of this particular ass. This letter, with its honestly faced doubts and its modesty, is highly characteristic of the writer. What he described as his "asinine" reluctance to influence events was deeply ingrained in his nature. He was now convinced that God did not want him to be Pope.

There is of course no telling what sort of Pope he would have made. We may be reasonably certain that he would not have been able to master the diplomatic intricacies of Papal politics. But then he would not have wanted to master them; he would no doubt have tried to turn the minds of his contemporaries from the political futilities of the day towards the eternal verities of the Church. And more: the example of his own life would have raised the religious prestige of the Papacy to long-forgotten heights. He might not have been a good *Pope* according to the standards set by his immediate predecessors, but he would clearly have been a *good* Pope, and that would have been an all-important new departure; in him, true Catholic Reform would have ascended the Papal throne. Instead, the tiara was worn by Julius III, neither a conspicuously bad man nor a conspicuously good one. The numerous sceptical observers of the Papacy (not all of them unfriendly) continued to doubt if Catholic Reform would come to anything at all.

Like his predecessors, Julius III could lay some of the blame for the condition of the Church on the secular rulers, but he made matters worse by direct participation in their contests, allying himself now with the Emperor now with France. When the hostile dynasties resorted to war again, in 1552, the Pope had no spiritual prestige to fall back on in the interests of peace. At this moment, rather late in the day, he asked Pole for advice on how peace could be restored. Pole's answer went straight to the root of the matter.[23] The series of wars between France and the Empire, he told the Pope, "must be attributed to the wrath of God, who uses them as a scourge for our sins, so that it is necessary to destroy the root by appeasing God, making peace first of all with Him; and thus we may subsequently hope for peace between the Sovereigns. The true way to do this is to bring about what for so many years has been so much desired by all pious men, namely reform." Just that pre-condition of outward peace Pope Julius III was not able to provide; he never pursued reform with anything like the zeal he devoted to gambling, banquets, and comedies.[24]

During Julius III's pontificate reform proceedings came almost to a standstill. Another session of the Council of Trent did indeed begin in May 1551, but owing to the outbreak of the war it had to be suspended a year later. The Church had to wait ten more years for the last and decisive session of that Council. In 1552 the prospects of reform seemed bleak indeed. Yet Pole did not despair: his faith enabled him to penetrate beyond the present and to anticipate in his mind what he was not destined himself to see. Soon after the second suspension of the Council he wrote: "It so happens that the day on which it was decided to suspend the Council was Good Friday. It seemed to me then as if I saw the dead body of Christ, of which the Council, representing the whole Church, is an image. Only a short time before the Council had evoked the brightest hopes of reform; now it seemed scourged with rods and dead, ready for the burial. Yet on that same day I was admonished to remember Christ's speedy return to life and all the other blessings which immediately followed His death, and then I was induced to conceive new hope for Council and reform."[25] Death and rebirth: he had had the experience himself and he had not forgotten its meaning.

Very little is known of Pole during these years: in itself an indication that his services were not often required at the Curia. (He was relieved from his governorship of the "Patrimonium Petri" in June 1550.) For a time he seems to have lived in or near Rome, and then, probably in 1553, he retired with his "familia" to the Benedictine Monastery of Maguzzano on Lake Garda, in Venetian territory. Did he intend to enter the religious life? We do not know, but it is quite possible. He did not, at any rate, feel settled. During these years he wrote an important letter to a Benedictine monk who had complained to him about the conflict between the menial duties of a monk and his desire for study and contemplation.[26] Pole tried to show him that the most menial duty, undertaken in the right spirit, can be a way of serving God. The Apostles, it is true, left their menial work, but only because they were called to preach the Word of God (Acts vi, 2); they left the "serving of tables" for a more laborious and more dangerous task. "I seek not my own will but the will of the Father": these were Christ's own words, and every Christian must try to realize them. A monk could be in no doubt about the "will of the Father": it meant doing what his superiors ordered him to do. And then, at the end of a long and painstaking letter, Pole adds: "Pray for me that I, who give you this advice, may be able to follow it myself. To tell you the truth, I am often perturbed by the same conflict."

The same old doubts again: how would he resolve them now? He could have entered an order, he could have devoted himself to the care of souls. It seems that he was unable to arrive at a decision. At this point, his "asinine" reluctance to do anything looks like a relapse into the indolence of his youth. Once again, he was waiting for a clear call. That call came at last, when in July 1553 the Princess Mary succeeded to the throne of England.

NOTES TO CHAPTER SEVEN

[1] The phrase is Fr. P. Hughes' (*Rome and the Counter-Reformation in England* (1942), p. 40. This book contains an excellent sketch of Pole's life.).

[2] Condivi's Life of Michelangelo (*Rime e Lettere di Michelangelo Buonarotti*, Firenze (1860), p. 145).

[3] *Q.*, vol. ii, p. 32 (May 1537).

[4] *Q.*, vol. ii, p. 141 (November 1538).

[5] Pastor, *History of the Popes*, vol. xi, p. 213 (cf. Pastor, op. cit., vol. xi, hapters. III and IV *passim*. Pastor's account, however, tends to be a little complacent on this and similar matters.).

[6] It is astonishing to find that even Contarini was in favour of this promotion (Pastor, op. cit., vol. xi, p. 184). Pole's letter of congratulation (*Q.*, vol. ii, p. 204) is mainly conventional.

[7] *L. + P.*, vol. xx, part 1, Nos. 292, 316, 394, 407, 408, 425, 552, 602.

[8] Pole, *De Concilio* (1562), fols. 69a, b.

[9] Transl. by Fr. V. McNabb, O.P. (*Dublin Review*, January–March 1936, pp. 152–9).

[10] *Concilium Tridentinum* (Görres—Gesellschaft), vol. xii (*Tractatuum Pars Prior*, ed. Schweitzer, 1930), pp. 664–85.

[11] Cf. *A. Treatie [sic] of Justification Found emong [sic] the writings of Cardinal Pole of blessed memorie* (Louvain, 1569). There is no reason to doubt the authenticity of this work which consists of an able exposition (in English) of the Tridentine decree. Gairdner made one of his very few mistakes when he wrote: "The theological views here expounded are in practical agreement with the reformers." (*D.N.B.*)

[12] Petyt MSS. 538, vol. 46, fol. 407b (Inner Temple Library, London).

[13] The sources for the history of this Conclave are discussed by Pastor, op. cit., vol. xiii, p. 2. I take most of the details from Pastor's masterly description (op. cit., vol. xiii, Chapter. 1). Cf. also H. Jedin in *Römische Quartalsschrift*, 1934, Bd. 42, pp. 306–9.

14 *S.P. Ven.*, vol. v, Nos. 587, 596.

15 *S.P. Ven.*, vol. v, No. 630.

16 *S.P. Ven.*, vol. v, No. 681. (On Pole's income, see Chap. 9, note 37.)

17 These were the words used by Pope Paul III between 1546 and 1549: *Archivio Storico Italiano*, Ser. V, vol. xxxv, 1905, p. 479. (For the date, cf. Pastor, op. cit., vol. xiii, p. 4.)

18 *S.P. Ven.*, No. 596. (Report by the Venetian Ambassador in Rome, Matteo Dandolo.)

19 Pastor, op. cit., vol. xiii, p. 14; *S.P. Ven.*, vol. v, No. 671.

20 *S.P. Ven.*, vol. v, No. 596.

21 Petyt MSS. 538, vol. 46, fol. 407b; *S.P. Ven.*, vol. v, No. 763. Cf. Petyt MSS. 538, vol. 46, fol. 402b–403b (in the course of a letter to Pope Paul IV, Caraffa): "Quod nunc [i.e. 1557] Sanctitas Vestra [i.e. Caraffa] coram universa ecclesia peperit, hoc in conclavi post mortem fe: re: Pauli Tertii concipere coepit." For the scene between Caraffa and Pole, cf. *S.P. Span.*, vol. ix, p. 483.

22 *Q.*, vol. v, pp. 53–65 (summarized in English in *S.P. Ven.*, vol. v, No. 671). Cf. *S.P. Ven.*, vol. v, No. 884. Pole's draft of this important letter (MSS. *Vat. Lat.* 5967, fols. 296 seq.) shows many corrections and alterations.

23 *S.P. Ven.*, vol. v, No. 737.

24 Pastor thinks that Julius III's efforts for reform have been underestimated, but not even on Pastor's showing do they amount to much (cf. Pastor, op. cit., vol. xiii *passim*).

25 *Q.*, vol. iv, pp. 71–2 (date supplied in *S.P. Ven.*, vol. v, No. 732: 30th July 1552). Seripando's view on the failure of Reform was equally gloomy: *Concilium Tridentinum*, vol. xiii (ed. Schweitzer and Jedin), n. 59. Seripando and Pole are borne out by H. Jedin, "Kirchenreform und Konzilsgedanke 1550–1559," *Historisches Jahrbuch*, 1939 (p. 418: ". . . diese in der Hauptsache richtigen Ansichten Seripandos").

26 *Q.*, vol. iv, pp. 21–9. The monk was Placido Contarini, Gasparo's nephew. The letter is undated; the contents and the tone suggest, I think, that it was written at this stage of Pole's life. The copy in MSS. *Vat. Lat.* 5967 is immediately followed by a letter written in 1553.

CHAPTER EIGHT

POLITICS AND RELIGION
(1553–1558)

POLE had not, of course, ceased to take a lively interest in the affairs of his native country. After Henry VIII's death (1547) he had exchanged some letters with Protector Somerset, but it had become increasingly clear that the boy-king Edward VI and his chief advisers were committing themselves to a Protestant policy. Mary's accession meant an unexpected change of scene. Pole received the great news early in August 1553, in his monastic retreat on Lake Garda. Without delay he sent a messenger to the Pope, with suggestions and advice. In an accompanying letter he expressed his hope that, together with Queen Mary, "there will be called to reign in that island justice, piety, and the true religion, which have hitherto been utterly crushed." A few days later he sent a letter to the new Queen herself. Mary, he wrote, could now, like the Blessed Virgin, sing the "Magnificat," and particularly the verse: "He has put down the mighty from their seat and has exalted the humble."[1] As used by Pole, these were no mere conventional words. God had spoken; His meaning was now beyond doubt. And Pole was immeasurably eager to interpret this meaning to the world at large.

At first, things seemed to go well. On his way to Rome Pole's messenger met a Papal emissary and returned with him to Lake Garda. The Pope had anticipated Pole's letter and had already appointed him legate for the affairs of England. The Papal instructions assured Pole of complete freedom of action: "We leave everything to your prudence, your learning, your charity, your zeal for the restoration and the progress of our religion."[2] Now for England! seems to have been Pole's first thought; at long last the end of his exile was in sight. But he had to learn patience, in the course of a particularly bitter year. Another Papal legate advised caution; the Queen herself was afraid of her cousin's premature arrival in England; the Emperor was opposed to Pole's journey; and the Pope was duly impressed by all these opinions.[3] The arguments put forward were all based on the unpopularity of Rome among the English people: the time for the arrival of a Papal legate, it was suggested, was not ripe, prudence demanded delay. Pole knew the exceptional difficulty of his mission to a country in which schism and heresy had had more than twenty years to take root, but he was profoundly convinced that this was not a case for the application of mere human prudence. "From my past experience in similar causes," he wrote to an over-cautious fellow-cardinal, "I greatly fear that the proceeding with too many worldly considerations in a cause in which God has so miraculously shown his power and goodness, may prove very injurious." And to the Queen he wrote in terms that could not fail to impress her devout mind: "I do not know if your councillors who urge you to set your kingdom's affairs in order first, and then restore religion, believe the words of the Gospel, saying that God watches over and governs even the smallest things, and that without Him no good can be accomplished. . . . The establishment of kingdoms is not founded upon mighty armies, or even upon human foresight, but their strength lies in God."[4]

The wisdom of the world and the wisdom of God: the politicians did not hesitate for a moment which of the two they should follow. One of them, a Papal nuncio, even remarked contemptuously: "[Pole] has really no experience of mundane things."[5] It may be that Pole was in too great a hurry to get back to England after his long exile, but the Emperor for one had a very special, all-too-mundane reason for not allowing him to return just yet — a reason of which the "inexperienced" Pole was quite aware.[6] This was the Emperor's plan to marry his son and heir Philip to the new Queen of England.

The Habsburg dynasty had always been, and remained for a long time, very fond of marriage-alliances. This marriage, it seemed to the ageing Charles, would secure to his son a decisive preponderance over the old rival, France. Having conceived his plan, he pursued it with his characteristic determination and astuteness. By the end of October 1553 he had succeeded in obtaining a solemn promise from Mary that she would become Philip's wife. It was generally taken for granted that Mary would not remain unmarried, but most of her subjects favoured her marriage to an Englishman. There were, however, very few eligible men, and the most obvious of them, Edward Courtenay, the son of the executed Marquis of Exeter, turned out to be a profligate. Was Pole among the candidates? Mary may have thought so; Pole did not; but the Emperor seems to have regarded him as Philip's rival. Pole's name had often been mentioned in diplomatic correspondence as a potential husband for Mary, and it is possible that this match had at one time been envisaged by Mary's mother, Katherine of Aragon.[7] Pole's remaining for many years in minor orders was also open to such an interpretation; he was still a deacon only and might have obtained a papal dispensation to marry.[8] Even if the Emperor was in the end convinced that Pole did not wish to marry,[9] so careful a schemer was not likely to leave anything to chance. Until the actual celebration of the marriage Pole had to be kept out of England, and kept out he was.

With regard to the Spanish marriage Pole was at one with the prevailing English opinion, which manifested itself in a particularly dangerous form in Wyatt's rebellion (January–February 1554). Pole told the Pope quite frankly that he could not "show himself favourable to this union, his knowledge of the national disposition convincing him that it was even more universally odious than the cause of religion."[10] And so it was; in this respect Pole showed greater mundane insight than the Emperor. Reconciliation with Rome was not popular, but neither were certain aspects of Edwardian Protestantism, and it is common knowledge that the Spanish associations of Mary's reign are partly responsible for the lasting estrangement of Englishmen from the Roman Church. Pole's earlier arrival might have made a difference.

Meanwhile the Pope had been completely won over by the arguments of the Emperor and his diplomats; it did not take much to convince Pope Julius III that one could not "swim against the stream." Pole was expressly and sharply told that he had to give active support to the Spanish marriage; to hinder it, the Pope added, would be harmful to the interests of religion and of the Holy See.[11] Julius III was hardly the man to lecture Pole on the interests of religion, and the latter remained unconvinced as to the merits of the Spanish match. In his answer he implied pretty clearly that he did not regard the Pope's command as compatible with the honour of God and the common good. For the rest, he either did not mention the marriage at all or continued to show that his feelings about it were, at best, lukewarm; his Imperial pension, it is worth noting, did not make him change his mind. As a consequence, he incurred the great displeasure of the Emperor who, on one occasion, virtually showed him the door.[12]

Repudiated by the Emperor and at cross purposes with the Pope, Pole withdrew to a monastery near Brussels, and in May 1554 he offered his resignation as a Papal legate. One of the Papal advisers, Cardinal Morone, reproached him for this step, suspecting that Pole was only too willing to withdraw from public business to the privacy of his studies. This suspicion, as we have noted so often, was not at all ill-founded, but in this case it was strongly repudiated by Pole.[13] It does seem, in fact, that Pole did not really wish to resign. True, he asked the Pope to find a more suitable legate, but that may have been merely a nominal request. There was, in fact, nobody who could have replaced him as legate for England; the Pope was bound to find that Pole was indispensable. By the summer the Emperor's wrath, too, began to subside, for the simple reason that at the end of July the marriage of Philip and Mary was celebrated, with all the appropriate pomp. After the ceremony the impressive new titles of the bride and bride-groom were proclaimed by a herald: "Philip and Mary, by the grace of God King and Queen of England, France, Naples, Jerusalem, and Ireland, defenders of the faith, Princes of Spain and Sicily, Archdukes of Austria, Dukes of Milan, Burgundy, and Brabant, Counts of Habsburg, Flanders, and Tyrol."

Two months later, on 21 September 1554, Pole wrote a dignified and vivid letter to King Philip.[14] "For a year now," the letter begins, "I have been knocking at the palace gate, and as yet nobody has opened it to me. If you ask 'Who is there?' I shall merely say: 'It is I who have endured expulsion from home and country for twenty years so that your consort should not be excluded from that palace with my consent.'" But Pole goes on to point out that he is not knocking in his own name, as a private person; he is knocking in the name of the successor of Peter, or rather in the name of Peter himself. When Peter had been liberated from Herod's prison, he knocked at Mary's door and she opened it to him (Acts xii). In England the supporters of Peter's authority were put in chains during the Herodian rule; now Peter is released once more and is knocking at the gate. But someone else as well is at the gate: Christ Himself. Mary, joined in the flesh to her husband, must now speedily open the door to Christ, her spiritual spouse. The new building must arise on the foundation stone of Christ. Otherwise the rain will descend and the floods will come, and the winds will blow and beat upon the house, and it will fall, and great will be the fall of it (Matt. vii, 27). (We may note in passing the frequency of Bible quotations in Pole's letters, a fruit of his Bible study; he anticipated this habit of his fellow-countrymen by a full century.)

Now that the main political obstacle had been removed Pole's knocking was at long last answered: Queen Mary was allowed by her domineering father-in-law, the Emperor, to invite Pole to England. On 13 November Pole set out on his journey from Brussels. Six days later he set foot on English territory in Calais. He embarked at once, and on the following morning

DOMINVS MIHI ADIVTOR

PAVLO IIII
P·O·M
ÆT·ANNO LXXXI
PONTIFICATVS
AVTE'M
ANNO III

POPE PAUL IV from an engraving by Beatrizet

Palatium Archiepiscopi Cantuariensis propè Londinum, vulgo Lambeth House.

LAMBETH PALACE IN 1647

from an etching by Wenceslaus Hollar

he landed in Dover where he was greeted by a personal letter from the Queen. A clerical orator, welcoming him at Canterbury, called him "Pater Patriae" and a "second Elias." His progress from Dover to Gravesend became a triumphal march: in the end he was accompanied by five hundred gentlemen on horseback. At Gravesend he was officially told that Henry's Act of Attainder against him had been reversed by Parliament. From here he continued his journey by boat, displaying the silver cross of a Papal legate. He landed at Westminster and proceeded at once to the Royal Palace at Whitehall (perhaps remembering a fateful visit to the same palace almost exactly twenty-five years before). At the gate he was met by King Philip; Queen Mary was waiting for him in the Hall. When the Queen saw him, we are told in a contemporary news-letter, "she turned to him and embraced him with the affection of a mother towards her son whom she had long given up as lost."[15] Then Pole presented his credentials and withdrew to Lambeth Palace across the river.

A few days after his arrival Pole addressed the two Houses of Parliament in the Queen's Presence Chambers at Whitehall. On the following day Parliament discussed his speech and drew up a petition asking the legate for the absolution of the Kingdom. And on Friday, 30 November, St. Andrew's Day, the final ceremony took place, again at Whitehall. The Lord Chancellor (Bishop Gardiner) read out the petition which was handed to the Cardinal by the King and Queen themselves. Then all who were present, including the King and Queen, knelt down, and Pole absolved them, as Legate of the Vicar of Christ, in the name of the Father and the Son and the Holy Ghost. Loud and repeated cries of "Amen" were heard from all sides; there were many tears. The scene, we are told, was particularly impressive because it took place in the evening, by the light of torches.[16] Almost at once a medal was struck to commemorate this unique occasion, showing England being raised from her knees by Pope Julius III in the presence of Philip, Mary, the Emperor, and Pole.[17] The medal has the air of perfect innocence. Looking at it casually one would not be led to suspect that the Emperor had delayed Pole's arrival, and with it this touching scene, for over fifteen months. Closer scrutiny reveals the stiffness and falsity of the gestures —possibly owing to the limitations of the artist or indeed to the discrepancy between the public spectacle and the underlying political reality. Pole, we must hope, may have forgotten his earlier troubles just for that day; it may well have been the happiest of his life. The reunion of England and Rome, he had written, "is and has been these many years my greatest desire, as it is my daily prayer to the only Lord and giver of all felicity";[18] now, at last, it was achieved. Two days later, after his solemn entry into London, the people of that city, the centre of English Protestantism, turned out in great numbers to receive his blessing.

The common people did not, at first, show any marked hostility to the restoration of Catholicism. The richer members of the community, on the other hand, had grave misgivings from the outset. They had obtained, by grant or purchase, many of the lands formerly belonging to monasteries, and the question of the ownership of this property ranked uppermost in their minds; social climbers do not relish the prospect of having to climb down again. This, too, Pole had realized from the very beginning. Pole did not suffer from any excessive optimism about English affairs; he was quite aware that a sea of troubles awaited him in England, worse than any he had hitherto experienced.[19]

Pole was, naturally, not particularly eager to condone the large-scale plunder of the Church that had been started by Henry VIII. His views can be gathered from a careful draft for his speech to Parliament (in the actual speech, it seems, he did not refer to this subject at all). "Albeit there were never so many Acts of Parliament," he intended to say, "yet could no man defend but it was sacrilege." Nevertheless, he was not going to suggest that all church goods should be returned, but he was determined to insist that the settlement must "not come in part of bargaining, . . . the return [to Rome] must be free and liberal." On this basis he favoured a settlement that would take due account of the persons who made "the foundation of their patrimony and living upon such lands," but he did not wish to be more explicit than that.[20] Very similar views he had put forward to the Queen a few months before ("obedientiam quasi precio comparare," he had written, must be strictly avoided), except that he had added his intention to decide each case on its own merits, bearing in mind the royal wishes. "Those who will be confirmed in their possessions," he declared, "should be indebted to their sovereigns for this benefit."[21]

This, of course, was the very thing the *nouveau-riches* of the Tudor age wanted to avoid at all costs; they did not wish to remain dependent on the benevolence of their sovereigns and were determined to obtain a secure title for their wealth by fair means or foul. It seems that Pole did not realize how many people had become accomplices in Henry's "ecclesiastical revolution." Religious opinions as such mattered little in this respect; the notoriously elastic human conscience enabled many to combine the acquisition of vast ecclesiastical lands with personal adherence to the Catholic Church. Take, for example, two of Mary's most diligent and influential Privy Councillors: Lord Paget, Lord Privy Seal, and Sir William Petre, a Principal Secretary. Both of them were Catholics, after a fashion, and the willing servants of a Catholic Queen, but both of them had amassed enormous wealth from the spoils of the monasteries and had succeeded in rising from humble origins to nobility and power. A close examination of the members of Parliament or the Justices of the Peace during Mary's reign would certainly yield many further examples of this kind. These "new men," of whatever religious presuasion, were bound to fear the worst in view of Pole's reluctance to confirm them in their possessions; the fact that he did not mention this question in his speech to Parliament must have seemed to them ominous.

As soon after Pole's arrival as practicable they made every

effort to get this matter settled. Both Houses of Parliament petitioned their sovereigns to obtain the necessary dispensations from the Papal legate. Pole was duly approached, and probably acting on the advice of Gardiner and the other leading statesmen, he issued the requested decree on 24 December 1554, according to which no possessor of Church property was liable to ecclesiastical censure, either then or afterwards. With all his intransigence, Pole was enough of a statesman not to endanger his main work, and he had at least carried his point that the question of the Church goods should be settled *after* the reconciliation with Rome. But the possessors of Church property still could not feel quite secure even now, for Pole steadfastly refused to absolve their consciences.[22] He remained of the opinion that they should voluntarily return their ill-gotten gains, and that they should not be allowed to regard themselves as free from sin unless they did so. So precarious a settlement might easily be overturned, for instance by a new Pope. This possibility, together with Mary's determination to return former Church property remaining in the hands of the Crown, contributed much to the growing unpopularity of her regime. Too many vested interests were endangered by the reconciliation with Rome.

Pole's position inevitably saddled him with great political responsibility. When Philip left England in August 1555, and again after the death of Gardiner, the Lord Chancellor, a few months later, Pole was asked to take over the official government of the country. He refused, but from now on he often left Lambeth Palace and joined the royal household wherever it happened to be. The Queen, according to the well-informed Venetian ambassador, wished that Pole should "have everything referred to him, it being evident that, whilst showing the utmost confidence in him, she distrusts almost all the others."[23] Pole was thus involved in a great deal of business and saw the Queen for two or three hours daily. The Venetian ambassador summed up Pole's position as follows: "It may in truth be said that he is both king and prince, though he exercises his authority so graciously and modestly as if he were the least of the Council, not choosing in any way to interfere, even in public affairs, except in such as are specially assigned to him."[24]

Among the matters on which Pole's advice was expressly sought was foreign policy. This was a subject that was bound to concern him in any case, as a Papal legate. Even before his return to England he had attempted to bring about peace between France and Spain, and in May–June 1555 he attended an unsuccessful peace conference at Calais. A few months later he was able to influence the more successful negotiations which led to a truce between the warring parties. This truce, however, like all its predecessors, was destined to be short-lived and soon afterwards England herself was, once again, drawn into the whirlpool of a European war. This disastrous sequence of events is inseparably connected with the dynamic personality of a new Pope.

Julius III died in March 1555. In the ensuing Conclave Pole was again regarded as a serious candidate. But this time he did not even go to Rome: immersed in the affairs of his native country and about to inaugurate his reform of the English Church, he now had no doubts at all that he was not required to stand for the Papacy. On 9 April Cardinal Marcello Cervini became Pope Marcellus II, but only three weeks later this great and good man suddenly died. On 23 May the Cardinals elected his successor: none other than Gianpietro Caraffa, the reformer and founder of the Theatines, who now called himself Paul IV.

Caraffa was already seventy-nine years old when he ascended the Papal throne. Tall, spare and sinewy, he still moved about with youthful vigour; he was never ill; and after a full day of public business he would sometimes read all night. He liked to take his frugal meals in the company of his familiars and often overwhelmed them with the torrents of his impassioned rhetoric. During such outpourings he was capable of saying the wildest things, but he was usually too proud to retract any of them, nor was anyone allowed to contradict him. As was to be expected in such a wilful and zealous man, he adopted the most exalted view of the dignity of his office. The secular princes, he thought, were his subjects; they had to sit at his feet and accept his decrees. It is significant that he put Dante's *De Monarchia* on the Index. To him, the medieval conflict between Church and Empire was of immediate reality and he intended to reassert the most extreme Papal claims of supremacy over all powers on earth. In the course of a few years he repeated the specific transgression of the medieval Papacy during its last stages: the pursuit of power at the expense of the spirit.[25]

On the face of it, it might seem surprising that Caraffa, a great and in some ways effective Church reformer, should have involved the Church in power politics. But the paradox can be resolved. Caraffa's unlimited belief in himself as the Vicar of Christ led him to identify all his own interests and fancies with the concerns of the Church; small wonder that he ended up by serving, not Christ, but only his petty self. He was all the more hopelessly lost in this extravagant identification since he could regard his life, from a narrowly religious point of view, as blameless. Like other fanatics of this kind, he created around himself a virtuous Inferno.

For our present purpose we must bear in mind that Caraffa was a Neapolitan. As such he was filled with burning hatred for the Spanish conquerors of Naples, the Habsburgs, and for all who supported them. Soon after his accession to the Papacy he began to prepare for war against the Habsburgs—for war, in the first place, of the Papal states against the Spanish power in Naples. This war broke out in September 1556, but what began as a conflict between two Italian states soon caused a large European conflagration. Philip was now King of Spain and ruler of the Netherlands as well as King of Naples (his father, Charles V, having abdicated in his favour early in 1556), and it did not take much to rouse the old enmity between the Habsburgs and their French rivals—that outstanding curse of the age. Very soon the Pope found a willing ally in France in his struggle against Philip; the Pope even went so far as to approve the attempt of his political advisers to enlist the help of the Turks against the Catholic King of Spain.[26]

Pole was bound to regard this war between the spiritual head of Christendom and the most powerful Christian king as the unmitigated disaster it actually was. Before the outbreak of war and for several months after its beginning he did all he could to bring about a peaceful settlement, by boldly addressing the sovereigns in the most serious terms. He repeatedly urged Philip to desist from any military action, and he wrote to the Pope: "A war between Your Holiness and King Philip must produce the gravest danger and harm to the whole Christian commonwealth." Only Satan, he went on, could have sown the seed of this dissension, and he added his belief (perhaps genuine and in any case enabling the Pope to save his face) that this estrangement must have been caused by the Pope's advisers.[27] To Cardinal Morone he complained that this quarrel was causing "the greatest grief in the minds of all good people here [in England], while the bad and perverse rejoice."[28] Morone did not dare to show this letter to the irascible Pope[29] who was already highly irritated by Pole's peacemaking activities. For several months the Pope did not communicate at all with his legate in England. Finally, in April 1557, at the height of his conflict with Spain, he withdrew all his nuncios and legates from Philip's dominions, and Pole was expressly deprived of his legatine power.

Meanwhile King Philip, after an absence of nearly two years, had at last returned to England and had easily succeeded in persuading his devoted wife to bring England into the war (it was this disastrous move that resulted in the much-lamented loss of Calais). Pole was now in an extremely difficult position: of the three sovereigns to whom he owed allegiance, two (Philip and Mary) were at war against the third (the Pope). Pole withdrew to Canterbury and for a time refused to see Philip in any official capacity; only as a private individual, under cover of darkness and alone, he paid him a courtesy visit.[30] But not even this extraordinary measure of tact could save Pole from the full force of Caraffa's wrath.

Caraffa's displeasure with Pole, at first obviously due to political reasons, soon changed its character; in his spiritual pride Caraffa was unable to distinguish between political opposition and sins against the Holy Ghost. An opponent of his foreign policy must, surely, be an enemy of Christ, in fact a heretic. The former Grand Inquisitor now remembered his earlier suspicions, which only a few years before he had solemnly withdrawn. [31] At first it was not clear whether the Pope had only cancelled Pole's legation or whether he wanted him to leave England and come to Rome. For a short time he chose to accept a moderate interpretation: Pole, he said, had merely lost the dignity of a "legatus a latere," retaining the legatine rank normally attached to the Archbishopric of Canterbury ("legatus natus"). But soon afterwards, in June 1557, he changed his mind. He nominated a new legate for England (a worthy but very aged friar called William Peto) and summoned Pole to Rome. At the same time he arrested Cardinal Morone, who had been closely connected with Pole, and handed him over to the Inquisition. What he now thought of Pole he disclosed in an extraordinary interview with the Venetian ambassador. On this occasion he talked himself into one of his paroxysms, inveighing against "that accursed school and apostate household of the Cardinal of England." Then he went on: "Why do you suppose we deprived him of the legation? You will indeed see the end of it; we mean to proceed, and shall use our hands. Cardinal Pole is the master, and Cardinal Morone, whom we have in the Castle, is the disciple, although the disciple has become worse than the master. Priuli is upon a par with these, and so was Flaminio who, were he alive now, would have to be burned." And then, after a good deal more of this, he made the most terrible statement of all: "If our own father were a heretic, we would carry the faggots to burn him."[32]

There can be no doubt whatever that if Pole had gone to

Rome he would have shared Morone's fate. (Morone, though the Inquisition failed to establish the charges against him, was not released from his imprisonment until after Caraffa's death.) As a matter of fact, Pole did not obey the Papal summons. Queen Mary, who was determined not to let him go, appealed to the Pope on his behalf, and when the Pope remained adamant she went so far as not to allow the messenger who was to bring the decisive Papal brief to land in England. Pole did not approve this course of action and refused to make any further use of his extraordinary legatine powers, but he attempted in various ways to justify himself before the Pope. He did so in an eminently dignified manner, in contrast to the Pope's virtually insane violence.

It was not easy for Pole to resist the highest representative of an institution to which he had devoted his life's work. He had his Scripture reference ready even for that (St. Paul's stand against St. Peter, Galatians ii, 11);[33] he knew, moreover, that the despotism introduced by Caraffa was injurious to Church and State. Yet Caraffa was now the Vicar of Christ; could a faithful son of the Church disobey his express command? He wrote a long apologia to Caraffa, but on re-reading this letter (a veritable treatise of eighty folio pages) he threw it into the fire and said: "Thou shalt not reveal the nakedness of thy father."[34] (Cf. Gen. ix, 22–3.) Instead, he sent several shorter letters and personal messengers to the Pope and his Secretary of State. The gist of his messages was this: England must have a legate. If the original legation cannot be restored, a suitable successor must be found. (Peto is not even mentioned in these documents: being in his dotage he was quite ineffectual.) Pole defends himself against the charge of heresy. He has worked hard for the restoration of the Catholic Church and the defeat of her opponents; does this smack of heresy? Can one suppose that he has done all this fictitiously? That, surely, would imply extraordinary impiety coupled with extreme ambition. And to ambition, Pole adds justly, "God has granted me the grace to show myself very averse during the whole course of my life."[35]

It so happens that a copy of Pole's undespatched letter to Caraffa survives. Must a Pope, is one of the questions Pole raises in it, be exempt from all criticism? No, is the firm answer, because a Pope is merely a man and can perform actions "quae non sunt Dei," and then it is the cardinals' duty in particular to admonish him freely. Never, Pole complains, has a cardinal been treated like this by any Pope. "But the Lord will answer for me," he states with confidence, "and the whole Church hears and understands what the judge, who is at the same time the accuser, does not hear at all."[36] Much of Pole's vindication takes the form of a personal appeal to Caraffa who had been his friend, and one passage has a poignancy all its own. Two men, Pole writes, he had worshipped ("coluissem") more than any others: King Henry VIII and Caraffa. One of them had deprived him of all his goods and all that was dear and pleasant in this life; the other now accused him of impiety.[37]

As Pole was writing this letter to his former friend, his mind went back to a scene that had occurred over twenty years before, on 21 December 1536, one day before the elevation to the purple of both Pole and Caraffa. It appears that Contarini and Giberti had suggested Caraffa for the cardinalate. At first the Pope had accepted this suggestion, but later he had changed his mind and chosen instead a far less worthy candidate (Aleander, then Archbishop of Brindisi). The night before the nomination day the Pope summoned Pole in the hope that he would confirm the intended change, owing to an altercation between Pole and Caraffa some days before. Pole, however, did nothing of the kind. He asked the Pope why he had changed his mind. After some hesitation the Pope informed him that he had reason to suspect Caraffa of impiety. Thereupon Pole lost his temper and drew the Pope's attention to the gulf that separated the worldly Aleander from the founder of the Theatines. Then he threw himself at the Pope's feet and implored him not to listen to the calumnies against Caraffa for whose piety he was ready to pledge his soul to the Pope and to the whole Church. After this dramatic interview the Pope returned to his first intention and Caraffa became a Cardinal on the following day.[38] Caraffa repaid Pole's disinterested service of friendship with blind and measureless hatred; Pole was fully entitled to speak of the "sword of grief" with which Caraffa had pierced his soul.[39] As Pole was survived by the much older Caraffa, he did not live to see the lifting of this heavy cloud.

NOTES TO CHAPTER EIGHT

[1] *S.P. Ven.*, vol. v, Nos. 764, 766.

[2] *Q.*, vol. iv, p. 109. For Pole's affairs in the years 1553–4, cf. the very reliable article by Dom R. Ancel in *Revue d'histoire ecclésiastique*, tom. x, 1909, pp. 521–36, 744–98.

[3] Cf. e.g. *S.P. Ven.*, vol. v, Nos. 771, 811.

[4] *S.P. Ven.*, vol. v, No. 786; *S.P. Span.*, vol. xi, p. 420.

[5] Quoted by G. Constant in *Revue des questions historiques* (1911), p. 601, from Vatican archives.

[6] *S.P. Ven.*, vol. v, No. 320.

[7] *Q.*, vol. v, p. 358. Cf. *S.P. Span.*, vol. v, part 1, p. 323; vol. v, part 2, pp. 199, 321; vol. xi, pp. 192, 207, 238.

[8] Cf. *L. + P.*, Addenda II, No. 1364; *S.P. Span.*, vol. v, part 2, p. 321; vol. xi, p. 192.

[9] *S.P. Span.*, vol. xi, p. 244.

[10] *S.P. Ven.*, vol. v, No. 856. The Emperor cannot have been ignorant of the English apprehensions: they were faithfully reported by his ambassador in a letter to Prince Philip, dated 3rd October 1553: *S.P. Span.*, vol. xi, p. 263.

[11] Cardinal Morone to Pole, 21st December 1553: Pastor, *History of the Popes*, vol. xiii, Appendix No. 21 b, pp. 448–9.

[12] *Q.*, vol. iv, pp. 133–8; *S.P. Ven.*, vol. v, No. 877. Was this the reason why his Imperial pension was paid so irregularly? (C.f. *S.P. Ven.*, vol. v, No. 611 note).

[13] *Q.*, vol. iv, pp. 133–7.

[14] *Q.*, vol. iv, pp. 162–6.

[15] *Copia d'una Lettera d'Inghilterra, nella quale narra l'entrata del Rever. Cardinale Pole.* This news-letter, on which most of this paragraph is based, is dated 30th November 1554, and was published in Milan on 24th December 1554. Internal evidence suggests that it was written by an Italian member of Pole's retinue; its details are corroborated by other evidence (e.g. *Q.*, vol. v, pp. 303–20).

[16] This paragraph is based on Dom R. Ancel's account (op. cit., pp. 794–5) which derives from an unpublished letter by Parpaglia, a member of Pole's household.

[17] Cf. illustration facing p. 144.

[18] MSS. *Vat. Lat.* 5968, fol. 128b (Vatican Library).

[19] Instructions for Parpaglia, August 1553 (Pastor, op. cit., vol. xiii, pp. 248–9, from an unpublished MS. in the Corsini Library at Rome); *Q.*, vol. iv, p. 137.

[20] MSS. *Vat. Lat.* 5968, fols. 118a, b, 120b. This codex contains four versions of Pole's speech to Parliament after his return; the last two (fols. 305a–359b, a monstrously long document, and 362a–376b, probably the actual speech) do not mention the subject of monastic lands. Cf. the contemporary report in the *Chronicle of Queen Jane*, Camden Soc., 1850, pp. 154–9.

[21] Bodleian MSS., S.C. 15673, pp. 35–7. The letter is dated "XI Augusti" and written "Ex Monasterio de Diligam" (i.e. Dilighem near Brussels, where Pole was in August 1554). This MS. is a later copy. I cannot trace the original, but the contents are corroborated by other evidence (cf. Ancel, op. cit., p. 779). The important passage towards the end: ". . . omnia hic processura, ut Ecclesiae scandalum vitaretur, Deus, ut par est et dignum, honoretur, possessores denique quibus Majestates vestrae satisfieri cuperent nihil haberent quod conquerantur imo hoc beneficium vestris Majestatibus deberent" (p. 37).

[22] He refused to add the clause: "Quod absque aliquo conscientiae scrupulo possent hujusmodi bona retinere": *S.P. Ven.*, vol. vi, part 1, No. 14. (Cf. 1 and 2 Philip and Mary, c. 8, secs. ix–xii.) It is significant that in 1556 Pope Paul IV ordered a "Processus super vero valore Ecclesiarum Regni Angliae," (cf. a copy of his brief in the P.R.O., Transcripts from Roman Archives, 9/68, ff. 359–60).

[23] *S.P. Ven.*, vol. vi, part 2, p. 1056.

[24] *S.P. Ven.*, vol. vi, part 2, p. 1070 (cf. *S.P. Ven.*, vol. vi, part 1, pp. 178–9). Pole never attended meetings of the Privy Council (*Acts of the Privy Council*, vols. v, vi).

[25] Many details in this paragraph are taken from Pastor's vivid characterization (op. cit., vol. xiv). This view of the medieval Papacy owes much to A. J. Toynbee's *Study of History*.

[26] Pastor, op. cit., vol. xiv, pp. 142–3. H. Pfeffermann (*Die Zusammenarbeit der Renaissancepäpste mit den Türken* (1946), pp. 210–29) exaggerates this sufficiently serious charge.

[27] *Q.*, vol. v, pp. 22–3 (cf. another letter to Paul IV, dated 7th December 1556, in *S.P. Ven.*, vol. vi, part 2, No. 753). Letters to Philip: e.g. *S.P. Ven.*, vol. vi, part 1, Nos. 526, 658. Some other Cardinals also tried to blame the Pope's advisers rather than the Pope himself for some of his misdeeds (British Museum, Add. MSS. 35830, fol. 22a); this is largely incorrect.

[28] Public Record Office, transcripts from Roman Archives, 9/68: ". . . ne gli animi di tutti boni qui grandissimo cordoglio, et all' incontro nei mali et perversi allegrezza" (14 July 1556).

[29] *Q.*, vol. v, p. 109.

[30] *S.P. Ven.*, vol. vi, part 2, Nos. 858, 880.

[31] *Monumenti di varia letteratura tratti dai manoscritti di Monsignor Ludovico Beccadelli* (ed. Morandi, Bologna, 1797–1804), vol. i, part 2, pp. 347–53.

[32] *S.P. Ven.*, vol. vi, part 2, No. 1067.

[33] *S.P. Ven.*, vol. vi, part 3, No. 1107; Petyt MSS. (Inner Temple Library, London), vol. xlvi, fol. 393a.

[34] *Q.*, vol. v, p. 387. There can be little doubt that a MS. in the Inner Temple Library, London (Petyt MSS., vol. xlvi, fols. 391–426) represents a contemporary copy of this letter (perhaps the copy Pole retained for his own use). On fol. 29 of the same volume the document is mentioned among the "Manuscripts out of John Fox his studye"; it may well have belonged to the martyrologist's vast MS. collections. Internal evidence suggests that the letter was written in or

after June 1557: Pole describes Mary's attempts to exclude the Papal messenger (April–June 1557), and Morone's imprisonment (31st May 1557) is mentioned. The handwriting is the same as that of several documents among Pole's Vatican MSS.; it is an Italian hand, probably belonging to one of Pole's secretaries.

35 *S.P. Ven.*, vol. vi, part 3, No. 1135. Cf. Petyt MSS., vol. xlvi, fol. 400b: "Hoc quidem facit eorum oblita quae pro ecclesiae obedientia deferenda ac restituenda feci legationem, in qua assidue cum haereticis pugnavi, ob huius ipsius criminis mihi abrogat." Pole's chief letter to Paul IV is in *Q.*, vol. v, pp. 31–6 (March 1558).

36 Petyt MSS., vol xlvi, fols. 414b, 391a, 411a (two folios are numbered "411"; this passage is on the first of the two): "Dominus pro me respondebit, et universa ecclesia audit et intelligit, quod iudex idemque accusator nullo modo audit."

37 Loc. cit., fols. 405a–b. There is no reason to doubt the sincerity of this feeling of veneration in both cases (cf. chap. 3., towards the end, and chap. 4 of this study).

38 Loc. cit., fols. 406a–407a (Pole hints at this occurrence in a letter to Caraffa's nephew: *S.P. Ven.*, vol. vi, part 3, No. 1107). Here is the crucial passage in full: "Cum causam [inquirerem?] cur sententiam mutasset, quam initio sermonis non exprimebat, sed grave quiddam significabat, tandem diceret fuisse impietatis suspicionem, quam sibi fecissent, quae de illa audisset; ad hoc quidem verbum sic exarsi, ut comparans Brundusinum [i.e. Aleander] cum Sanctitate Vestra [i.e. Caraffa] modestiae fines, quod postea sensi, transirem in Brundusino vituperando, ut pietatem Sanctitatis Vestrae laudarem. Denique proieci me ad Pontificis pedes suppliciter orans, ne ob talem causam, quae sine dubio calumniandi causa ficta esset, sententiam mutaret eligendi Sanctitatem Vestram, pro cuius pietate auderem animam meam ipsi et ecclesiae oppignerare."

39 *Q.*, vol. v, p. 34.

CHAPTER NINE

REFORMATIO ANGLIAE
(1555–1558)

POLE who had devoted so much time in exile to the Catholic reform movement, was not likely to forget this main concern of his life when he returned to his native country. What others regarded simply as the restoration of the religious *status quo* was to him something rather different: a renewal springing from that spirit of reform which he had helped to arouse in the Catholic Church. He did not envisage a return to the state of things before the divorce of Henry VIII; in the light of the "Consilium de Emendanda Ecclesia" these good old days appeared far from good.

Pole started the reform in the only adequate way: by convoking a national synod, on the strength of his legatine capacity. In November 1555 the bishops and clergy of both Provinces, "who usually attend provincial synods,"[1] were asked to come to London. Their first meeting was on 2 December and they continued to meet for two months, sometimes at Westminster and sometimes at Lambeth. Pole's thoughts may well have gone back to the even more significant, though smaller assembly he had presided over at Trent almost exactly ten years before. Once again it fell to him to make the opening speech, and once again he attempted to stir the consciences of his listeners, this time in his native tongue.[2]

"Whereas every year," he began, "by the custom of the laws of the Church the archdeacon is wont to visit or to send for the priests under his charge, this I thought best to be done in my presence that have the cure over all, which am come to know and see the cheer of my flock." Then he went on to stress

142

the terrible responsibility that fell on priests: to answer for
their own souls as well as for the souls of their flock—a charge
"which no man that can tell what he does, would ever take
except for obedience to the highest pastor of all." And then
followed a strong indictment: the pastors had failed in their
duties and had caused the religious upheavals of the last
decades. They had failed chiefly in two ways: by ignorance
and by covetousness. Pole knew enough about the widespread
ignorance of priests to make this statement, though he may
not have known that of about 300 priests examined a few years
earlier in the Diocese of Gloucester, 170 were unable to repeat
the Decalogue and 27 could not even say who wrote the
Lord's Prayer.[3] Such ignorance, Pole maintained, was the
natural breeding-ground of heresy. Similarly, the heretics
could "win the feeble sort . . . [by] putting before their eyes
the abuses, and specially covetousness, of the priests." This
covetousness, a heritage of man's depraved nature, had to be
held in check by salutary laws, and to draw up such laws was
the aim of the synod. Pole concluded his short and powerful
address in a characteristic manner by reminding his listeners of
Judgment Day—"that terrible day when everyone shall appear
before [the judge] to render count both of word and deed, and
according to that to receive his meed. Who is it that does not
tremble when he hears of that day? What saint is in this world
that does not fear that day when he looks on himself?"

After this warning the synod set to work and produced its
decrees with commendable speed. These decrees leave no
possible doubt about the ills of the Church and the remedies to
be applied. All pastors must reside among their flocks—or else
how can they minister to their needs? They must be severely
punished for absence, and pluralists must confine themselves to
one benefice forthwith. Heretical books must not be printed,
sold, or read. To counteract the spread of false doctrines all
priests, including bishops, must fulfil their preaching duties and
instruct their congregations in the principles of faith. But
preaching is not enough: example is even more important.

Priests, and bishops in particular, must avoid all outward pomp such as precious clothes or exquisite furniture; their fare must be frugal and sparing. They must use a large part of their revenues for charitable and educational purposes. They must, of course, remain unmarried and be above any suspicion of unchastity. Much more care must be used in the selection of candidates for the priesthood: colleges must be founded, from which, as from a seed-bed ("seminarium") future priests can be selected by the bishops. The "abominable crime of simony" demands the severest punishments: deprivation and excommunication. Finally, these decrees must be enforced by frequent and searching visitations.[4]

All this sounds familiar. It is nothing but a restatement of the "Consilium de Emendanda Ecclesia," of the programme of the Italian reformers with whom Pole had been so intimately associated. In addition, the synod began to prepare a new book of homilies, a catechism, and an English translation of the New Testament. An English prayer-book for private use had already been published (in June 1555).

The synod was adjourned in February 1556 and never met again; a little over a year later Pole lost his legatine powers and could no longer hold a legatine synod. But in March 1556 Pole became Archbishop of Canterbury (two days before his consecration he was, at long last, ordained priest), and in January 1558 he held a convocation of his own province. That assembly produced a new set of reforming decrees, confirming and amplifying the first.[5] In the meantime Pole had to see to it that his decrees, unlike so many others of this kind, should be enforced. This could only be done by visitation, both in his own diocese and throughout his province.

A metropolitical visitation was carried out in 1556. Not much information about it has come down to us, but one document relating to the Diocese of Lincoln shows very clearly that Pole was faced with a Herculean task. Many priests of the diocese had married during the previous reign (one of them was still living with his wife); others, after leaving their wives, had

MARY TUDOR

from a medal struck to commemorate
the Restoration of Catholicism

VITTORIA COLONNA
from a medal

PIETRO BEMBO
from a medal

CARDINAL POLE

from a painting by Sebastiano del Piombo

resorted to them again; and yet others had fled and left their benefices vacant. There was altogether an alarming number of vacancies, for a variety of causes, and many churches were nearly in ruins. Among the parishioners there was a good deal of impatience with ceremonies and a tendency to mock at them, but—and this is worth noting—not much evidence of positively Protestant views came to light. Heresy-hunting was not, in any case, among the aims of this visitation which was meant to fulfil Pole's promise to Parliament: "I am come not to destroy, but to build; to reconcile, not to condemn."[6]

The outlines of the "Reformatio Angliae" had now been fixed. Its ultimate success was bound to depend on the quality of the new prelates and priests. It is hardly surprising that Pole, during his short régime of not quite four years, was unable to raise the general level of the clergy; a great part of the priests, according to a contemporary observer, resented Pole's reforms and "wished the Cardinal back again in Rome,"[7] and in the next reign most of them (perhaps three-quarters) conformed without resistance. Still, Pole's efforts were not without result: a considerable body of ordinary priests remained loyal to Catholicism, and a large number of those who outwardly conformed remained Catholics at heart and secretly continued to administer the Catholic rites.[8] It was altogether easier to renew the ranks of the bishops, and in this respect Pole was eminently successful. All bishops, except one, stood firm when challenged by Elizabeth's government and had to be deprived of their sees. Among these steadfast bishops were many who had been consecrated during Pole's tenure of office. These were the men Pole had chosen for the carrying out of his far-reaching reform plans —serious and learned men, altogether different from the worldly prelates so predominant in the preceding reigns. One of these men deserves particular mention, both for his own sake and for the sake of his friendship with Pole: Thomas Goldwell, Bishop of St. Asaph.

Goldwell had left England during the time of Henry's schism and had attached himself to Pole's household in Italy, suffering

attainder together with Pole and his family in 1539. He was a
member of the Viterbo "spirituali,"[9] and in 1547 he entered
the newly founded, particularly severe order of the Theatines.
He remained, however, in close contact with Pole, whom he
attended during the dramatic conclave of 1549–50 and again
from September 1553 onwards; he was present at Pole's death-
bed. His former master would not have disapproved of the way
in which he spent the rest of his life (fully twenty-five years).
Refusing all ecclesiastical preferment he devoted himself to the
spiritual duties of a Theatine, and for a time served the great
St. Charles Borromeo, Archbishop of Milan. It is absurd to
suggest, as a recent writer has done,[10] that he was "accustomed
to soft living": that was not what Theatines and associates of
Borromeo could get accustomed to. A contemporary reference
to him, by William Cecil, as a "very simple and fond man"[11]
may be nearer the mark, in the sense that a truly religious man
will always appear in this light to men of the world. Goldwell,
who was so intimately connected with Pole, was bound to be
considered a simpleton by the same people who despised Pole
for his lack of "mundane experience."

With such bishops working under him Pole could hope to
revive the English Church. In addition, there was of course a
good deal of administrative work to be got through. As Archbishop of Canterbury Pole had to administer any diocese in his
province during a vacancy.[12] As a Papal legate, he was liable
to be asked for absolutions or dispensations by all who wanted
to be on the safe side; a surprising number of applicants, for
example, discovered that they had a natural horror of fish or
some other disability and could therefore not fast in Lent.[13]
More important were Pole's efforts to transmit to the people
the spirit behind his reforms, by preaching. In one of his
sermons, which was addressed to the citizens of London, he
censured the spirit of the age much in the manner of his celebrated adversary, Hugh Latimer. "When," he asked, "was
more excess of meat and drink than now? More excess of
sumptuous apparel, both in your bodies and in your houses;

the churches remaining bare, robbed and spoiled? When was less alms given? . . . [I exhort] you to enlarge your hand more to the help of the poor, that are so dear to Christ, that he says, whatsoever is given to them in his name, he takes it as given to himself. . . . In Italy, in two cities only, there is more alms given to monasteries and poor folks in one month than in this realm in a whole year."[14]

Monastic alms were now particularly needed because of the attempted restoration of some of the dissolved monasteries. "From day to day," wrote the Venetian ambassador, "through Pole's exertions, hospitals, monasteries, and churches rise from the ruins."[15] The Franciscans returned to Greenwich, the Dominicans to Smithfield, the Benedictines to Westminster Abbey, the Carthusians to Sheen. Pole himself took part in the ceremony by which the Carthusians of Sheen were restored to the monastery where he had spent his boyhood.[16] Further restorations were planned, for instance at Canterbury and Glastonbury, but not achieved.

One of Pole's greatest difficulties was the scarcity of suitable priests. For this reason alone, if for no other, he had to take an active interest in the state of the two universities which, until the establishment of the proposed seminaries, would train all priests. He sent a commission to Oxford and Cambridge, who were to carry out a legatine visitation on his behalf (he was also Chancellor of both universities). Cambridge had been a hotbed of Protestantism, but most Cambridge dons accepted the new régime without resistance; Oxford had been and remained staunchly Catholic. Pole produced a set of strict and salutary reform regulations, but this was not, unfortunately, the only result of this visitation. The visitors indulged in the unpleasant pastime of digging up heretical corpses: after some sort of trial they exhumed and burned the bodies of Martin Bucer and a German colleague of his, and they exposed on a dunghill the remains of Peter Martyr's wife, a former nun. The best that can be said about these outrages is that they were confined to the dead. But these proceedings were bound to arouse disgust or ridicule, and it is difficult to see what good could have been expected of them.

More serious even than this was Pole's failure to achieve an adequate reform of the academic curriculum. Here, a weakness in Pole's intellectual equipment became noticeable (a weakness which we have already noted in a different context). Pole was not securely grounded in theology and was therefore not properly qualified for this task. The result was distinctly poor: Aristotle, Porphyrius, and Agricola were the only permitted text-books for logic, Aristotle alone for moral and natural philosophy: in theology, attention was to be evenly divided between the Bible and a text-book, the chief authority being none other than the twelfth-century *Liber Sententiarum* by Peter Lombard, a collection of the "sentences" of the Fathers.[17] Unable to recognize the merits of books which he had not studied, Pole fell back on a "safe" summary of the Fathers, ignoring Aquinas along with the scholastic hair-splitters of the later Middle Ages, expelling Duns together with the dunces. The absence of Plato among the prescribed philosophical authors is even more remarkable in view of Pole's own intellectual formation.

It may be that Pole, owing to his outstanding debt to the Scriptures, was inclined to place so much confidence in Bible study as not to be too particular about the choice of text-books. But he knew himself that these matters were not quite so simple as that. He assured the London Synod, for example, that the word of God was contained not only in the Scriptures but in secular writings as well. On that occasion he went on to proclaim: "Truth, no matter who pronounces it, comes from the Holy Ghost."[18] In the light of this invaluable conviction, borne out by so much else in Pole's life, his academic reform is bound to appear disappointing.

Pole's "Reformatio Angliae" as a whole cannot be judged by results; the time was too short and what Pole achieved was undone by his successors. Some critics of Pole have blamed him for being sluggish in the performance of his duties.[19] Pole could have pleaded in his defence the hampering reliance of the Queen on his advice and the futile conflict with Paul IV. But it is true that Pole's reforms progressed at a rather leisurely speed: bishoprics were often left vacant for a long time, the visitation of his diocese took several years, and nothing at all seems to have been done about priests' seminaries. This applies to Pole's political activities too. Never fond of administration, he was quite unable, in his decline, to impart vigour to the conduct of public affairs. His innate tendency towards inaction may also, to some extent, explain his role in the notorious persecution of heretics, which has overshadowed his more constructive endeavours.

This persecution—no other name will do justice to the facts —has given rise to much speculation. The question of the responsibility for it has been discussed again and again, but in this general form the problem may be insoluble. There can be no doubt that nearly 300 people were burnt in the course of not quite four years, but they suffered a few at a time or singly, in many places (not only in Smithfield), under many authorities, and for a variety of causes. No one ever decided that there must be a holocaust of heretics; we are faced with a series of haphazard proceedings, not with a planned campaign.

To obtain a clear view of the Marian persecution is not at all easy; Foxe's *Book of Martyrs*, like a great mountain range, lies between us and the facts. Not that many of Foxe's facts are wrong: a large number of them have withstood all scrutinies. But Foxe does obscure the vision by his tone and his propagandist devices, and even more by the essential uniformity of his martyrs. He failed to recognize that the martyrs did not all belong to the same category. Some of them had committed outrageous acts of violence, including murder and sacrilege. Then there were the prominent Protestants, chiefly Cranmer, Latimer, and Ridley, who were bound to be proceeded against. Cranmer and Ridley, moreover, had engaged in treasonable activities in connection with Northumberland's conspiracy and could have been executed on this count. They and Latimer were, in fact, burned for heresy, and their heroism at the stake is justly famous, but if they had been the last victims, or even if the persecution had been confined to recalcitrant clerics, it would not have provided material for what has rightly been called "a saga cycle, a great folk-legend."[20] This could only come about by the extension of these proceedings to the laity, and particularly to the common people.

At the beginning of Mary's reign many of the Protestant gentry and clergy were allowed to leave the country, and many others conformed, as they had conformed before and would conform again. Compliance, though of course not limited to these classes of the population, was fairly easy for them; the common people were much more exposed to the activities of officials, both lay and clerical. The vast majority of the victims came from the lower classes: artisans, labourers, husbandmen, their wives and widows (sixty of them), and even their children. The following story from Foxe sheds a vivid light on the distress of these simple people.[21]

Four women of Essex were denounced by their local Justices of the Peace and sent up to Bishop Bonner of London, who administered to them his usual set of nine articles in order to test their faith. The second of these articles reads: "Item that thou the said N. in times past hast also believed, and so dost believe at this present, that there are in the Catholic Church seven Sacraments, instituted and ordained by God, and by the consent of the holy Church allowed, approved, received, kept, and retained." All the women answered that they did not know how many sacraments there were, and one of them "had heard that there was one Sacrament, but what it was she could not tell." On the other hand, they were quite sure that "Christ's natural body is in heaven and not in the sacrament of the altar" and that "the Mass is an Idol." One of the women—a girl in her 'teens—said quite simply that when she was eleven years old she "began to learn the faith set forth in King Edward's days." It is obvious that these women, insofar as they were clear about their beliefs, were utterly dependent

on the religious teaching that had been widespread ever since
Henry's breach with Rome and legal during Edward's reign.
And this is true of nearly all the victims.

The legal machinery of the persecution was fairly simple.
The foundation was the revival of the old heresy laws by
Parliament in December 1554. In addition, Royal commissions
were issued in some (perhaps all) dioceses, charging selected
groups of clerics and laymen with the repression of heresy and
sedition.[22] On the basis of these acts and commissions various
officials began to present suspects to the bishop of the diocese.
In many cases it is not clear who were the prime movers, but
it is not necessary to assume the existence of many anonymous
heresy-hunters. There were some who tried to cover up earlier
lapses of their own by redoubled zeal, and there were some busy-
bodies about (there always are), but other officials may not have
done more than their plain duty. The cases were naturally most
numerous in the strongly Protestant areas of England: London,
East Anglia, Sussex, and Kent (i.e. in the dioceses of London,
Norwich, Chichester, and Canterbury). Only one execution
each is recorded north of the Trent and west of Salisbury. Of
the bishops concerned, it is Bonner of London who has been
saddled with the worst reputation by Foxe and other historians,
but it does not seem that he was a particularly bloodthirsty man.
He was faced with the fact that his busy diocese produced some
of the busiest heretics, and on several occasions he had to be
spurred into action by letters from the Queen or the Privy
Council.[23]

And Pole? The redoubtable Foxe, summing up Pole's
attitude, wrote: "Although it cannot be denied by his acts and
writings, but that he was a professed enemy, and no otherwise
to be reputed but for a Papist: yet again it is to be supposed,
that he was none of the bloody and cruel sort of Papists."[24]
We remember, in fact, that Pole's leniency in Viterbo had got
him into trouble in Rome. Only a few months before his return
to England he wrote to a German friend: "We must deal with
heretics in such a manner that a certain note of paternal love

151

remains in all our sentences; though they are our avowed enemies, they are still our children and must be treated as such."[25] We may gather from this passage that Pole was not exactly pleased with the Roman Inquisition, and he did not hesitate to say so to the Grand Inquisitor himself. In the course of a long conversation in Rome, in April 1553, he told Caraffa that "he did not like the methods of the Inquisition, even though he agreed with its aim."[26] "A Papist, but not a bloody Papist": Foxe's judicious verdict was taken over by other anti-Catholic historians, and it may be allowed to stand. How then, we must ask, could this persecution come about while Pole was in high office?

Pole, it must be realized, shared the conviction held by contemporary Catholics and Protestants alike that heresy was the anti-social crime *par excellence.* He told the citizens of London that "there cannot be a greater work of cruelty against the commonwealth than to nourish or favour [heretics], . . . who, as it were, undermining the chief foundation of all commonwealth, which is religion, make an entry to all kind of vices in the most heinous manner."[27] Pole was not included in the Royal heresy commission for Canterbury, but he issued two commissions himself, in July 1556, and March 1558,[28] both of them to his archdeacon and other officials, who were to act on his behalf. "With bitterness of heart," he wrote in his second commission, "we understand that heretical opinions are propagated in our city and diocese. At this we cannot connive: therefore we appoint you to examine the suspected, the detected, the denounced, the accused, and give them up to the secular arm, if the badness of the case so require."[29] "With bitterness of heart": we may well believe that Pole was surprised by the stubbornness of the Protestant opposition. His experience with Protestants or waverers in Italy had been altogether different. In that country his natural leniency had worked tolerably well; in England he was confronted with heresy in a form and on a scale unknown to him. Soon after his return to England he is said to have recommended leniency, remarking that "there was a great difference to be made between a nation uninfected, where some few teachers came to spread errors, and a nation that had been overrun with them, both clergy and laity."[30] If Pole ever said this, he either forgot it again or was too weak to give expression to it in his policy. Instead, he avoided facing the issue and allowed inferior officials to act in his name, not often inciting them to action, but not often willing to hinder them either. His occasional, haphazard clemency can hardly be said to matter very much.[31]

This failing deserves careful analysis. We know that Pole was capable of considerable fortitude; he could, on occasions, stand up to anybody, including kings and popes. In this case, however, he was evidently not clear in his own mind where his duty lay. The principle itself was not in doubt: he believed that heresy was punishable by death, though he was not fond of inquisitorial methods. But should the principle be applied in these cases? Among those who thought that it should be applied was the Queen, Pole's sovereign, kinswoman, and friend.

Pole's behaviour could not but be influenced by his close friendship with Mary. The Queen seems to have placed unique confidence in him, and it was entirely for her sake that Pole, who disliked courts, spent so much time at her Court. When Pole arrived in England, Mary told him that she felt as much joy as on her accession to the throne.[32] In Pole, a part of her youth was returning to her: the son of her governess and the faithful adherent of her mother. He alone, of all comparable persons, had had nothing to do with the humiliations and trials of her life. As King Philip made it only too obvious to her that their union was nothing but a *mariage de convenance*, she clung to Pole as her only real friend. It would have been cruel of him not to respond to this desperate attachment, but he need not have gone so far in adopting his friend's point of view (a mistake he was by nature inclined to commit). Mary, contrary to her text-book reputation, was not cruel, but Protestantism seemed to her a danger to Church and State alike; the heresy commissions issued in her name made no attempt to distinguish between heresy and sedition. And in her growing isolation she tended to exaggerate the dangers of sedition, especially after Wyatt's revolt.

It was folly to take the uncoordinated activities of Protestant labourers and artisans as seriously as the real rebellions and conspiracies of those years. Mary was unable to see that, and Pole, it seems, did not see it either. Here, the politicians among his critics would have been really justified in censuring him, but they did not show more insight themselves.[33] In this way Pole, who had suffered so much from the unfortunate alliance of politics and religion, became himself entangled in a mistaken identification of religious and political aims. Some words of Priuli's, written in a different context, can be applied to Pole: "How dangerous are the favours of great princes, even to those who with their whole heart are proceeding in the path of piety for the service of God."[34] Throughout his life Pole had struggled against the political misuse of religion; now, towards the end of it, he was not strong enough to oppose the use of secular power at the cost of breaking the second of the two commandments on which "hang all the law and the prophets."

The persecution which began early in 1555 was still in progress nearly four years later when the lives of both Mary and Pole were drawing to an end. Pole, though only fifty-eight, was worn out by care and prematurely old. In 1558 a contagious fever was raging in England and claimed many victims; by September of that year Pole was a very sick man. On 4th October he made his will.[35] He appointed sole heir and executor his intimate friend Alvise Priuli, "whose piety," he added, "and singular fidelity and love I have observed and tested for more than twenty years which he has spent in the closest union with me." Priuli, who was not himself in any financial need, was to distribute Pole's estate among the latter's poor kindred, friends, and servants, and for charitable purposes. Pole's list in which he specified these bequests is not extant; it must have been very long, for Priuli stayed on in England for a whole year after Pole's death in order to fulfil his dead friend's wishes.

Rumours had got about that Pole had received vast treasures from Queen Mary and that he must therefore be fabulously rich. This was not so; Priuli was not even sure whether all legacies could be met. In earlier years Pole's income had not been large. During the last few years of his life, when his resources were more ample, his personal requirements remained very modest,[36] but he increased the number of his familiars and the size of the other liabilities of his office. Thus, in just under two years (from January 1556 to November 1557) he received and spent about £16,000.[37] His first biographer says justly: "He was not eager for wealth; what he had, he spent, and he gave gladly. He wished his 'familia' to be well treated; he avoided all debts and made his expenditure accord with his income."[38] When death approached he was therefore unencumbered by possessions or debts and could devote himself to a more important concern.

On 15 November Pole received extreme unction from Thomas Goldwell. The Queen was also dangerously ill and two days later, at 7 a.m., she died. The members of Pole's household intended to withhold the news of her death from their master, but one of them forgot and told him. What followed must be reported in the words of Priuli who was present.[39] "On hearing it, after remaining silent for a short while, he then said to his intimate friend, the Bishop of St. Asaph [Thomas Goldwell], and to me that in the course of the Queen's life and of his own he had ever remarked a great conformity, as she, like himself, had been harassed during many years for one and the same cause, and afterwards, when it pleased God to raise her to the throne, he had greatly participated in all her other troubles caused by that elevation. He also alluded to their relationship, and to the great similarity of their dispositions. . . . His right reverend Lordship then remained quiet and silent for about a quarter of an hour, but though his spirit was great, the blow nevertheless, having entered into his flesh,

155

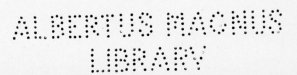

brought on the paroxysm earlier, and with more intense cold than he had hitherto experienced, so that he said he felt this would be his last. He therefore desired that there might be kept near him the book containing the prayers which are said for the dying. He then had vespers and compline said as usual, which part of the office yet remained for him to hear; and this was about two hours before sunset—in the morning he had heard Mass also, as was his daily custom. In short it was evident that as in health that saintly soul was ever turned to God, so likewise in this long and troublesome infirmity did it continue thus until his end, which he made so placidly that he seemed to sleep rather than to die." His death occurred twelve hours after the death of the Queen.

About a month later Pole's remains were buried, according to his request, in the chapel of St. Thomas à Becket in Canterbury Cathedral, where they are still. A simple inscription, which has since disappeared, marked the spot: "Depositum Cardinalis Poli." His household was quickly dissolved; Priuli followed him to the grave after less than two years. Within a very short time most of his friends and adherents found themselves in prison or in exile. His cause was about to be defeated in his native country, his life-work seemed to have been in vain.

NOTES TO CHAPTER NINE

[1] Wilkins, *Concilia Magnae Britanniae* (1737), vol. iv., p. 131.

[2] MSS. *Vat. Lat.* 5968, fols. 1–4 (Vatican Library). I have modernized the spelling and punctuation.

[3] *English Historical Review*, January 1904.

[4] The legatine decrees in the form in which Pole read them to the Synod on 10th February 1556 can be found in Wilkins, op. cit., vol. iv, pp. 121–6. Pole revised and amplified them, and sent the second version to Rome where it was published in 1562 under the title "Reformatio Angliae." I summarize from the final version.

[5] Wilkins, op. cit., vol. iv, pp. 155–68.

[6] Foxe, *Acts and Monuments* (8th edition, 1641), vol. iii, p. 110. The findings

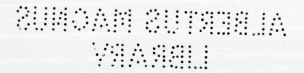

of the Lincoln visitation (a fascinating document) can be found in Strype, *Ecclesiastical Memorials* (1816), vol. vii, pp. 237–63.

[7] *Cal. S.P. Domestic*, 1547–80, p. 74 (Sir John Masone to Courtenay, 15th February 1556).

[8] Cf. P. Hughes, *Rome and the Counter-Reformation in England* (1942), pp. 146–8. This book also contains short accounts of Pole's bishops: pp. 85–95.

[9] "M. Thomaso inglese che si fece theatino." Estratto del Processo di Pietro Carnesecchi (ed. G. Manzoni, *Miscellanea di Storia Italiana*, tomo x, 1870), p. 254.

[10] Evelyn Waugh, *Edmund Campion* (second edition, 1947), p. 90.

[11] *Cal. S.P. Foreign*, 1561–2, p. 563.

[12] Cf. Pole's Archiepiscopal Register at Lambeth, fols. 37a–64a.

[13] Cf. Pole's Legatine Register at Douai (microfilm at Lambeth), *passim*.

[14] Strype, op. cit., vol. vii, pp. 340–65. The two Italian cities are probably Venice and Florence. There are two sets of English sermons by Pole in MSS. *Vat. Lat. 5968*.

[15] *S.P. Ven.*, vol. vi, part 1, No. 150.

[16] *S.P. Ven.*, vol. vi, part 1, No. 704.

[17] Wilkins, op. cit., vol. iv, p. 158.

[18] MSS. *Vat. Lat.* 5966, fols. 55a–55b: "De Materia verbi quae ad aedificationem ecclesiae pertinet. . . . Ad materiam enim verbi pertinet quicquid vel ad corripiendum vel ad instruendum pertinet, ut perfectus sit homo ad omne opus bonum perfectum. Hoc autem hauritur non solum ex sacris libris, quamquam ex illis praecipue, quam ex ethnicorum libris . . . a quocumque veritas dicitur a Spiritu Sancto est." (This passage occurs among documents relating to the London Synod; it may have been written for a different purpose.)

[19] *Q.*, vol. v, pp. 69 seq.; R. W. Dixon, *History of the Church of England* (1891), vol. iv, *passim*. (Dixon, however, minimizes the importance of the visitations and overlooks Pole's legislative activity in Convocation, January 1558.)

[20] P. Hughes, op. cit., p. 104.

[21] Foxe, op. cit., vol. iii, pp. 701–2 (Bonner's articles: p. 612).

[22] The commission for the diocese of Canterbury is contained in Pole's Archiepiscopal Register at Lambeth, fols. 17a–18a. It can also be found in the *Calendar of Patent Rolls, Philip and Mary*, vol. iii, pp. 24–5. It does not contain Pole's name, but this may be due to his other commitments. On these commissions, cf. Dixon, op. cit., vol. iv, pp. 573–4.

[23] Dixon, op. cit., vol. iv, pp. 363, 371, 398.

[24] Foxe, op. cit., vol. iii, p. 785.

[25] *Q.*, vol. iv, p. 157.

[26] Morandi, *Monumenti di varia letteratura tratti dai manoscritti di Monsignor Lodovico Beccadelli* (1797–1804), vol. i, part 2, p. 351.

[27] Strype, op. cit., pp. 343–4.

[28] Pole's Archiepiscopal Register at Lambeth, fol. 20b; Wilkins, op. cit., vol. iv, pp. 173–4.

[29] Translation (abbreviated) from Dixon, op. cit., vol. iv, pp. 714–15.

[30] Burnet, *History of the Reformation* (3rd edition, 1731), vol. ii, p. 222. Burnet does not give his authority, but it is unlikely that he would have invented these words. Other parts of the same passage fit in well with what we know Pole to have said or written. Cf. also Foxe (op. cit., p. 118) who reports that Pole exhorted the bishops early in 1555 "to win the people rather by gentleness than by extremity and rigour."

[31] Foxe, op. cit., vol. iii, pp. 708, 785, 786.

[32] *Q.*, vol. v, p. 309.

[33] I do not wish to take part in the controversy regarding the sincerity of the famous sermon by Alfonso a Castro, King Philip's adviser and author of a treatise on the punishment of heretics. The fact remains that neither King Philip nor his father nor their advisers made any serious and persistent attempts to stop the persecution in England.

[34] *Q.*, vol. v, p. 351 (*S.P. Ven.*, vol. vii, No. 80).

[35] *Q.*, vol. v, pp. 181–7. Cf. Priuli's letter, *S.P. Ven.*, vol. vi, part 3, Nos. 1286, 1287, 1291, 1292.

[36] His wardrobe, for example, was remarkably small: M. Haile, *Life of Pole* (1910), p. 544.

[37] M. Haile, op. cit., p. 533. For Pole's household in England, cf. Strype, op. cit., vol. vii, pp. 76–7. Here is a short summary of Pole's financial position after his student days: Until 1537 he received an income of £263 17s. 10d. per annum from his ecclesiastical benefices in England (*Valor Ecclesiasticus* of 1535, published in 1810, vol. i, pp. 261, 272, 326; vol. ii, pp. 76, 295, 296). His income after 1537 was derived from various sources: a Papal salary of 2,400 scudi per annum while he was living in Rome; the revenues of the governorship of the Patrimonium Petri from 1541 to 1550 and of the abbacy of Gavello (800 scudi per annum) from 1549 onwards; after 1543 a legacy from Bishop Giberti of 2,800 ducats per annum; and some years later an Imperial pension on the see of Burgos amounting to 2,000 ducats per annum (a consolation prize for the loss of the Papacy?). The last two items, however, were paid irregularly: *S.P. Ven.*, vol. v, No. 681 note. After his return to England Mary gave him two grants amounting to £4,100 per annum (*S.P. Ven.*, vol. vi, part 3, No. 1287). The value of the Archbishopric of Canterbury (inadequate like all stationary incomes owing to the great rise of prices) was just over £3,000 (according to the *Valor Ecclesiasticus* of 1535). In addition, the Queen gave much property to the Church, but that, according to Priuli, did not form part of Pole's income (*S.P. Ven.*, loc. cit.). His annual income for the years 1556–7 was apparently about £8,000 (see above in the text). On this subject, cf. also *Q.*, vol. v, pp. 383–4.

[38] *Q.*, vol. v., p. 383.

[39] *S.P. Ven.*, vol. vi, part 3, No. 1286.

CHAPTER TEN

FAILURE AND FULFILMENT

AS Pole lay dying in Lambeth Palace he may well have thought of his life as a failure: the future of the English Church once more uncertain—the reform of the universal Church unsettled—he himself suspected of heresy by the reigning Pope. Perhaps he felt then what another English Catholic, Gerard Manley Hopkins, was to express much later, at the end of another seemingly futile life:

> . . . birds build—but not I build; no, but strain,
> Time's eunuch, and not breed one work that wakes.

We, too, cannot help seeing his life as a failure if we confine ourselves to Pole's intervention in English affairs. His book against Henry VIII, his various diplomatic missions, his zealous activities during the last five years of his life—none of these could prevent the utter defeat of the Catholic cause in England. Pole's reputation in his native country has suffered accordingly. If "Popery" is indeed the evil thing so many Englishmen believe it to be, so staunch an adherent of the Papacy cannot hope to be held up as a pattern to English schoolboys. Froude, the influential historian and great prose-writer, carried the day in the nineteenth century with his description of Pole as outdoing even foreigners in cunning, in contrast to the homespun honesty of Henry VIII. Some shadows have since been added to the generally accepted picture of that monarch, and Froude's picture of Pole no longer carries so much conviction as it once did, but Englishmen still regard Pole with a good deal of suspicion. Even when he is not hated, he is little understood. An exile most of his life, he has remained an exile after death.

This is not the place to argue the merits of the English separation from Rome. Some rejoice at it; to others it is a disaster; no Christian can think of it with indifference. But on one of its aspects a measure of common agreement can be reached: its immediate influence on ecclesiastical reform in England. Pole's "Reformatio Angliae" could not take root owing to the reversal of ecclesiastical policy after his death. As a result, Elizabeth's Church became the only unreformed Church in Europe. The Protestant Churches had given expression, in varying degrees and different ways, to their ideas of reform; the Church of Rome had carried out a thoroughgoing spring-cleaning; but the Elizabethan Church remained unpurged. Whatever may be said of "Good Queen Bess," one can hardly think of her as a religious figure. The main concern of her ecclesiastical policy was the safe subjection of the Church to the temporal power (combined with the continued pillaging of Church property); to remedy the glaring abuses that had crept into the Church of England (as they had done elsewhere) was not in Elizabeth's interest as she conceived it. Many of the Elizabethan prelates were respectable enough, but hardly any were filled with genuine religious zeal. The Archbishop who succeeded Pole (Matthew Parker) was a cultivated don and administrator but a man of little spiritual power. Pluralism and absenteeism among the clergy remained widespread. This state of languor lasted until the early seventeenth century. Then the overdue reform was taken in hand simultaneously by two divergent movements: by the High Anglicans and by the Puritans. The Puritan movement eventually led to the growth of nonconformity outside the Established Church. Would the unity of the Anglican Church have been preserved, one wonders, if the necessary reforms had been carried out under Elizabeth? Be that as it may: it is in any case very regrettable that the sound principles of Pole's reforms were neglected for such a long time.

The "Reformatio Angliae" and the restoration of Catholicism in England were clearly failures. But this is not all that can be said about Pole's life-work. It is all too easy to echo the insular charge put into the mouth of Gardiner in Tennyson's *Queen Mary*:

> You, my lord, a polish'd gentleman,
> A bookman, flying from the heat and tussle,
> You lived among your vines and oranges,
> In your soft Italy yonder! You were sent for,
> You were appeal'd to, but you still preferr'd
> Your learned leisure.

"Learned leisure": that takes no account of Pole's strenuous efforts for Church reform abroad, from the "Consilium de Emendanda Ecclesia" to his part in the Council of Trent and his uncompromising advice, whenever it was required, to two successive Popes. The presence of Pole in the College of Cardinals helped to bring about such measure of reform as was achieved in the twenty years after the "Consilium." That there was not more of it was due to causes beyond Pole's control.

"Learned leisure," then, is not a fair description of Pole's life in Italy after about 1534. But there is an aspect of his life abroad that may well cause some surprise. Why, we must ask ourselves, did not Pole follow the example of his friends Giberti and Sadoleto in devoting himself to the cure of souls? Pole preferred the secular administration of the Patrimonium Petri and was not ordained priest until two years before his death (until then he was a deacon). We have noticed that his refusal to take full orders aroused the suspicion of some observers who jumped to the conclusion that Pole did not want to prejudice his claims to the throne of England. Nothing in Pole's character or record suggests that this suspicion was justified. Why then his reluctance to become a priest? Was it due to an exaggerated sense of his own unworthiness, something like his old Oxford tutor's "immodest modesty"? Or was it connected with his almost morbid fear of public office? It rather looks as if it had been the latter. If so, we must count this fear of the priesthood among his weaknesses. But it should be remembered that, in a sense, he did have the cure of some souls: not only his famous friends of whose spiritual troubles we have been allowed to catch an occasional glimpse (Vittoria Colonna, for example, or Flaminio), but the more reticent members of his household such as Alvise Priuli, Bartholomeo Stella, Thomas Goldwell, and faithful servants like Bernardino Sandro and George Lily. These men were prepared to follow Pole wherever he went, and admired his character and his learning.[1] To them, and indeed to a much wider circle all over Europe his way of life meant much. Here, at last, was a Prince of the Church who was not eager for power and had no taste for worldly pomp. In the midst of so much gaily accepted corruption, Pole's life must have put courage into many hearts.

Such an example was all the more important in view of the great difficulties which the Catholic reform movement had to face. At first, the reforming cardinals were in a small minority. Such reform activities as those of Giberti in Verona or of the Theatines in various places required time to bring forth the expected fruit. Then there were the various political difficulties which first postponed the calling of a Council, and then hindered its work. The Popes themselves were not consistently helpful: Paul III and Julius III vacillated, and Paul IV spoilt much by his uncontrolled passion. It was not until about 1570 that the moral regeneration of the Papacy and the Roman Church as a whole had made decisive progress. The Popes from Pius IV onwards, supported by a new generation of excellent prelates, saw to it that the decrees of the Council of Trent, which had at long last been concluded in 1563, should not remain on paper. Residence of bishops and priests was enforced; seminaries for the education of the clergy were founded (here, Pole's London decree of 1556 served as a pattern); the liturgical ceremonies were everywhere performed with renewed vigour and care; and saints like Charles Borromeo, Philip Neri, or Teresa of Avila set an inspiring example to the people at large. The post-tridentine Church of Rome experienced a genuine revival—the kind of revival that Pole had been steadfast enough to believe in when the Church seemed dead.

Nobody would want to diminish the fame of the later reformers and saints. But it is only fair to add that this revival might have been much more difficult or much longer delayed but for the life-work of a small band of early reformers: Contarini, Giberti, Caraffa, Gaetano di Tiene, Pole. By the time the Jesuits began their work (1540), these men had already mapped out Church reform and begun to lay its foundations. To have belonged to such a group, to have prepared such a fulfilment, cannot possibly be called failure, even though the fruits were gathered after Pole's death. In the history of the Roman Church Pole plays a very important part; from the point of view of that Church it may even be regarded as a providential part.

Though Pole had been under a cloud during Caraffa's pontificate, his memory was quickly rehabilitated after Caraffa's death (1559). The Church, as Pole had confidently anticipated, understood the rights and wrongs of his case. Between 1562 and 1569 several of his works were published in Rome, Venice, and Louvain, some of them with official backing. Among those who contributed to the clearing of his name was the great Augustinian, Cardinal Seripando, one of the Papal legates at the final session of the Council of Trent. In a letter written two years after Pole's death Seripando speaks of Pole's "sanctity and innocence of life, his gentleness in condemning others, and the compassion he showed to those whose human frailty had made them fall." Pole himself, Seripando went on, had never been in need of such compassion, "being always irreproachable in word and deed."[2] An exaggerated account, no doubt, but one which suggests that Seripando looked up to Pole as an ideal, and this view was shared by some of the best of Pole's contemporaries.

"Gentleness in condemning others" ("mansuetudine in condennar' altri"): this remained Seripando's aim, and among those who brought about the triumph of Catholic reform there were other disciples of Pole. But—and this is a very important qualification—Caraffa's spirit had by no means vanished from the Catholic Church. "Nothing fails like success": the revived Catholic Church was now able to counter-attack the Protestants (it is in this sense only that the term "Counter-Reformation" is appropriate), but some of the most successful weapons employed in this counter-attack were such as to distort the original impetus behind the revival. Only considerations of this kind will enable us to grasp the exact historical significance of Pole's life. We must therefore try to clarify this issue as best we can.

What was it that fundamentally separated Pole from Caraffa —that even prevented them, in the end, from understanding each other's language, in a worse-than-Babylonian confusion of tongues? That, surely, was their different relation to human-ism. We have been at pains to point out, in the course of this study, what wide divergences of outlook are covered by the term "humanism." Contarini and More were humanists; but so was Bembo. Behind More, but ostensibly behind Bembo too, stood Erasmus. Caraffa refused to make any distinctions. To him, Erasmus was the arch-villain, and therefore he put all works of Erasmus on the Index, even those, he expressly stated, "which contain nothing against or about religion."[3]

This is all the more remarkable as Erasmus' practical concern was identical with Caraffa's: the revival of religion. Part of the way the two could, and did, go together; Caraffa, too, was interested in good editions of the Greek Fathers. But soon they came to a point where they parted company. It is not at all easy to indicate this point. In looking for it we may be helped by recalling the fundamental convictions of that great Christian humanist, Gasparo Contarini: the belief that human reason plays an indispensable part in interpreting and supplementing revelation, and the related belief that men, as rational beings, are free in the sense that any authority over them must be based, not on arbitrary will, but on reason. Reason and Freedom: both of them derive here from a certain trust in man

164

—in man not as man, but as the likeness, in spite of grievous blemishes, of God. The highest part of man, we are told by Erasmus, is an "image of the Divine mind," "quaedam Divinae mentis imago."[4] And the law of freedom, as Contarini does not fail to add, is the law of Christ: the trust in one's fellow man is the secular counterpart to Christian charity.[5]

All this was not, of course, a discovery of the Christian humanists of the Renaissance; it was nothing but the conscious restatement of a great Christian tradition. This tradition is embodied, for example, in the Offertory of the Roman Mass—a text that all these men must have heard and said hundreds of times: "Deus qui humanae substantiae dignitatem mirabiliter condidisti et mirabilius reformasti"—"O God who hast wonderfully created, and still more wonderfully restored, the dignity of human nature." This can be expressed in many different ways; Contarini knew the teaching of Thomas Aquinas better than Erasmus did, and he could therefore formulate these matters more clearly and more comprehensively. But he shared Erasmus' attitude to the chief intellectual issue of their age: both of them, and More as well, attempted to accommodate the results of the newly stimulated learning within the framework of the newly stimulated Christian religion. A man like Contarini was bound to be utterly dismayed when he became acquainted, in the course of his diplomatic journeys, with the workings of the Spanish Inquisition.[6]

Not so, as we have seen, Caraffa. His lack of charity is too obvious to need any comment. But here we are mainly concerned with the secular counterpart to this failing: his persistent distrust of other people. Caraffa was unable to master his overbearing temperament; the chaos of his Papacy was merely an outward expression of his inner chaos. This unreasonable man may well have found it difficult to trust the reason of others. And his example was contagious; the Counter-Reformation proceeded more on Caraffa's lines than on Contarini's.

It would of course not be true to say that the Counter-Reformation owed nothing to humanism. The Jesuits, for example, made extensive use of the Greek and Latin classics in their famous schools; Catholic scholarship produced such valuable works as those of the historian Baronius; Cardinal Bellarmine, the author of the revised Vulgate, was a truly and widely learned man. Pole had his later successors as well as Caraffa, but they were seldom in decisively influential positions, and all the time Index and Inquisition kept their watch. When the next challenge came—science—the ultimate response was similar to Caraffa's rejection of humanism. First Erasmus, then Galileo: the principle was the same. And so was the consequence: the divorce, increased by later encounters and still painfully noticeable in our time, between the best secular thought and the Catholic Church.[7]

In the history of this conflict a place of honour is due to Reginald Pole, along with Erasmus, More, and Contarini, even if Pole, less interested in theology than the other members of this group, was sometimes inclined to underrate the value of human reason. In Pole's time, Bembo represented a distorted humanism, Caraffa a distorted Christianity; in his best moments Pole realized that a divorce between humanism and Christianity makes both of them lose their true nature. This is an aspect of his life that transcends the realm of the purely biographical, though it is securely rooted there. Christian humanism is not a ready-made formula one can fall back on, but an ever-present task; the study of the lives of Christian humanists is an integral part of this task:

> We are born with the dead.
> See, they return, and bring us with them.[8]

Such an intimate relationship need not blind us to human weaknesses. "Tout comprendre" is *not* "tout pardonner"; one can try to comprehend everything, even succeed in doing so to a large extent, and yet condemn the wilful transgression or the culpable negligence. "If we lower our standards in History," was Lord Acton's prophetic warning," we cannot uphold it in Church or State." In arriving at our verdicts we must of course use the judicial experience gained in self-examination; any form of self-righteousness is out of place. We shall not condone the rack or the stake, but we shall remember the concentration-camps; we shall not excuse the shirking of moral responsibility, but we shall not forget how often we have turned our backs on our own duty. Pole's chief temptation, we know, was to escape from public duties to his study and oratory and to the warm company of his friends. Sometimes he overcame this temptation and sometimes he succumbed to it. The greatest blot on his memory, his part in the Marian persecution, was caused by this particular weakness. He was certainly not a heresy-hunter, but he did nothing to stop the persecution. While he was sitting back, much indescribable suffering occurred. It is irrelevant to point to similar sufferings caused by the opponents of Pole's cause, here and abroad: a hundred wrongs never make a right, and this was a wrong.

Too often, however, Pole is remembered for nothing but this wrong, or the weakness that caused it. Enough has been said to suggest that this is really not the whole story. We must also remind ourselves that, owing to his part in the Catholic reform movement, he was able to take a firm stand against the dangers of the modern State. In claiming room for the newly revived religious forces he was bound to set a limit to the insatiable Leviathan. It is this stand that should secure Pole a hearing in our time. There is no other refuge, we have learnt, except religion, but that refuge can become a veritable fortress if it is built with the seriousness and care of men like More and Pole. The sphere of inwardness, they knew, must be safeguarded against the brutal attacks of secular power, and if the State invades this sphere, no natural loyalties must prevent determined resistance against this outrage. No one would claim that Pole was always successful in this resistance, but there can be no doubt that he tried to perform this task to the best of his ability. And he was among the few men of his time who fully realized the significance of this issue.

We cannot go further than that. Much of his life must necessarily elude us: we cannot listen to his meditations and prayers, we cannot recapture the full quality of his intense religious life. But something that is closely related to that side of him has appeared again and again in the preceding pages: his genius for friendship.

Wherever he was, at all stages of his life, he was immediately surrounded by friends. Some, no doubt, were attracted by his princely rank and by hopes of preferment. But there cannot have been many such even in the beginning, and later his worldly prospects were not bright enough to attract place-hunters. Many people felt real, unforced love for him. This love comes out in the pages of his first biographer; in Sadoleto's and Contarini's letters; in letter after letter written by an astonishing number of people (we have been able to notice only a few of them). It seems that Pole, who did not feel at ease in public, could quickly establish significant relations with people when he met them in a small group. In his student days he had the reputation of being taciturn, but he seems not to have retained this habit in later life. We are told in fact that his conversation was animated and gay; "having seen much of the world and read much, he could entertain anybody in a pleasant manner."[9] But entertainment was only the surface; his friends went deeper in serious dialogue, in common spiritual exploration. We have no direct records of these meetings; we can only infer their quality from the character of those who took part in them. Let us recall some of their names for the last time: Contarini, Sadoleto, Flaminio, Vittoria Colonna. It was in the company of these friends that Pole was happiest and at his best. And here we will leave him.

NOTES TO CHAPTER TEN

[1] Cf. Priuli's enthusiastic account of Pole's lectures on the Pauline Epistles (*Q.*, vol. ii, pp. civ–cv), and Beccadelli's similar views in his biography, *passim* (*Q.*, vol. v). For a hostile report of the admiration accorded to Pole, cf. *L + P.* Addenda II, No. 1364: "Many worship Pole for a god" (report by one of Cromwell's agents, Padua, 22nd October 1538).

[2] H. Jedin, *Seripando* (1937), vol. ii, p. 637 (this book is now available in an American edition). Dr. Jedin emphasizes Pole's decisive influence on Seripando's life.

[3] F. H. Reusch (ed.), *Die Indices Librorum Prohibitorum des 16. Jahrhunderts* (1886), p. 183. The Index of Pius IV (1564) mitigated the sentence by confining the ban to the following works of Erasmus: "Colloquiorum liber, Moria, Lingua, Christiani matrimonii institutio; De interdicto esu carnium, ejusdem Paraphrasis in Matthaeum." But it was added: "Caetera vero opera ipsius, in quibus de religione tractat, tamdiu prohibita sint, quamdiu a facultate theologica Parisiensi vel Lovaniensi expurgata non fuerint" (Reusch, op. cit., p. 259).

[4] Erasmus, *Opera Omnia* (Leyden, 1704), vol. v, fol. 772e, quoted in R. Pfeiffer, *Die Einheit im geistigen Werk des Erasmus*, Deutsche Vierteljahrsschrift, vol. xv (1937), pp. 473 seq.

[5] For Contarini's views, see Chapter 4 of this study. It might be thought that in this context I am alluding to Dostoevsky's parable of the Grand Inquisitor. I am not; Dostoevsky uses a different concept of "freedom" (cf. Romano Guardini's analysis in his book on Dostoevsky). I hope to develop this view of Christian Humanism in a forthcoming study on the Erasmian Idea.

[6] F. Dittrich, *Gasparo Contarini* (1885), p. 111.

[7] For an earlier stage of this conflict, cf. Philip Hughes, *A History of the Church*, vol. iii (1947), pp. 112–24.

[8] T. S. Eliot, *Little Gidding*.

[9] *Q.*, vol. v, p. 385.

NOTE ON THE SOURCES

IN the course of studying a subject of this kind one comes to feel gratitude and affection for the scholars and antiquarians who have done so much to prepare the ground. In anything that concerns Cardinal Pole pride of place belongs to Cardinal Quirini who, between 1744 and 1757, produced *Epistolarum Reginaldi Poli S.R.E. Cardinalis et aliorum ad ipsum Collectio* (published in Brescia, in five volumes). This work contains the bulk of letters from and to Pole; additional letters from other sources do not greatly alter the picture that emerges from this collection. Quirini's work also contains some of Pole's other writings (e.g. his "Apologia ad Carolum Caesarem"), as well as the first biography of Pole by Lodovico Beccadelli, who knew Pole well and accompanied him on some of his diplomatic missions. The work of two English scholars supplements Quirini's: James Gairdner's unparalleled *Letters and Papers of Henry VIII*, and Rawdon Brown's *Calendar of State Papers, Venetian* (of which vols. v and vi contain the largest collection of Pole's letters outside Quirini's book). Other *Calendars of State Papers* (Spanish, Domestic and Foreign) also have references to Pole.

Unpublished materials of biographical value are rather scarce. Pole's *Episcopal Register* preserved at Lambeth and his *Legatine Register* preserved at the Municipal Library of Douai (a microfilm of which is deposited at Lambeth) do not yield much biographical information; their evaluation would, however, be interesting for the history of ecclesiastical administration. Then there are the Vatican MSS. concerning Pole (mainly in Vat. Lat. 5964, 5966, 5967, and 5968; microfilms of all these are now in the Bodleian Library at Oxford). Vat. Lat. 5964 and 5966 contain various reform treatises by Pole, with traces of repeated corrections and alterations, of value chiefly for the history and background of the Catholic reform movement. Vat. Lat. 5967 consists mainly of letters (or their drafts) nearly all of which are in Quirini. Vat. Lat. 5968 contains only

English papers: sermons, homilies, a treatise on the Sacrament
of the Altar, a speech to the London Synod, speeches to
Parliament and their elaborate drafts. Some other papers
relating to the London Synod are in Vat. Lat. 5966. (It
must be added that portions of these codices are illegible in
microfilm, owing to the state of the MSS.) According to
Pastor, there are some unpublished letters of Pole's in the
State Archives of Parma; I have not been able to receive
a reply from that institution which is said to have suffered
in the recent war. Finally, there are some relevant documents in various English libraries and archives: at the Public
Record Office among the Transcripts from the Roman Archives;
in the British Museum (especially Add. MSS. 15388 and
35830); in the Bodleian Library (especially S.C. No. 15673),
and in the Inner Temple Library, London (Petyt MSS., No.
538, vol. 46). The last named is of great importance and
should certainly be published in full (it is Pole's undespatched
great vindication of himself to Pope Paul IV).

There is no need to specify the other materials, both primary
and secondary. As far as England is concerned, Conyers
Read's *Bibliography of Tudor History* is very serviceable, and
Pastor's *History of the Popes* provides extensive and excellent
bibliographies for anything that concerns Pole's work abroad.
(More recent publications can be found in the relevant periodicals and in the bibliographical notes attached to the various
articles in such encyclopedias as the *Lexikon fur Theologie und
Kirche* or the *Dictionnaire de Théologie Catholique*.) Nor is this
the place for the discussion of the very varied biographies of
Pole (by T. Phillips, W. F. Hook, A. Zimmermann, M. Haile,
R. Biron and R. Barennes, and others). One biographical sketch,
however, must be mentioned here, because its accuracy marks
it out as an ideal starting-point for any inquiry about Pole:
James Gairdner's article in the *Dictionary of National Biography*.
With three exceptions (mentioned below: Chapter 1, note 20,
Chapter 5, note 22, and Chapter 7, note 11) all the facts con-
tained in that detailed account appear to be entirely correct.

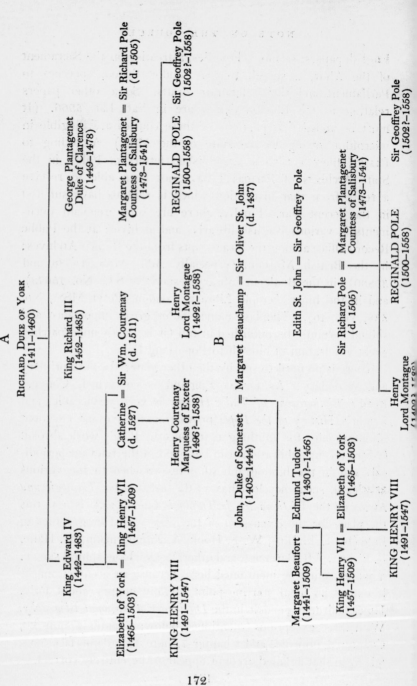

A

RICHARD, DUKE OF YORK
(1411–1460)

King Edward IV
(1442–1483)

King Richard III
(1452–1485)

George Plantagenet
Duke of Clarence
(1449–1478)

Elizabeth of York = King Henry VII
(1465–1503)   (1457–1509)

Catherine = Sir Wm. Courtenay
(d. 1527)

Margaret Plantagenet = Sir Richard Pole
Countess of Salisbury   (d. 1505)
(1473–1541)

KING HENRY VIII
(1491–1547)

Henry Courtenay
Marquess of Exeter
(1496?–1538)

Henry
Lord Montague
(1492?–1558)

REGINALD POLE
(1500–1558)

Sir Geoffrey Pole
(1502?–1558)

B

John, Duke of Somerset = Margaret Beauchamp = Sir Oliver St. John
(1403–1444)   (d. 1487)

Margaret Beaufort = Edmund Tudor
(1441–1509)   (1480?–1456)

Edith St. John = Sir Geoffrey Pole

King Henry VII = Elizabeth of York
(1457–1509)   (1465–1503)

Sir Richard Pole = Margaret Plantagenet
(d. 1505)   Countess of Salisbury
(1473–1541)

KING HENRY VIII
(1491–1547)

Henry
Lord Montague
(1492?–1558)

REGINALD POLE
(1500–1558)

Sir Geoffrey Pole
(1502?–1558)

172

INDEX